KNITTING
WITH
RIBBON
YARN

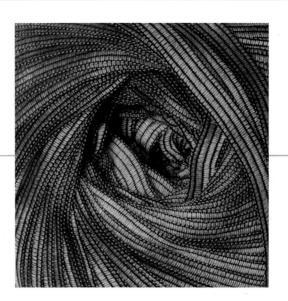

KNITTING
WITH
RIBBON
YARN

TRACY CHAPMAN

SEARCH PRESS

A QUARTO BOOK

Published in 2006 by Search Press Ltd
Wellwood
North Farm Road
Tunbridge Wells
Kent TN2 3DR
United Kingdom

Copyright © 2006
Quarto Publishing plc

ISBN 1 84448 140 9

A catalogue record for this book is
available from the British Library.

Conceived, designed, and produced by
Quarto Publishing Plc
The Old Brewery
6 Blundell Street
London
N7 9BH

QUAR.KTY

Project editor: Trisha Telep
Designer & art editor: Sheila Volpe
Photographers: Sian Irvine, Martin Norris
Assistant art director: Penny Cobb
Pattern checker: Eva Yates
Text editor: Pauline Hornsby
Proofreader: Claire Waite Brown
Indexer: Diana LeCore

Art Director: Moira Clinch
Publisher: Paul Carslake

Manufactured by Provision Pte Ltd,
Singapore
Printed by Star Standard Industries (PTE)
Ltd, Singapore

CONTENTS

USING RIBBON YARNS AS A FABRIC

CORE TECHNIQUES

THE PROJECTS

Classic sleeveless
shell top **42**

Halter-neck camisole
with crochet flower **45**

Luxury shawl **48**

Short-sleeved
raglan top **51**

Halter-neck
back-wrap top **54**

Designer wrap **56**

Classic round-neck
cardigan **58**

Sleeveless polo-neck
pullover **62**

Super casual
single-button vest **65**

Long-sleeved
wrap-front sweater **68**

Ultra feminine
camisole top **71**

Summer poncho **74**

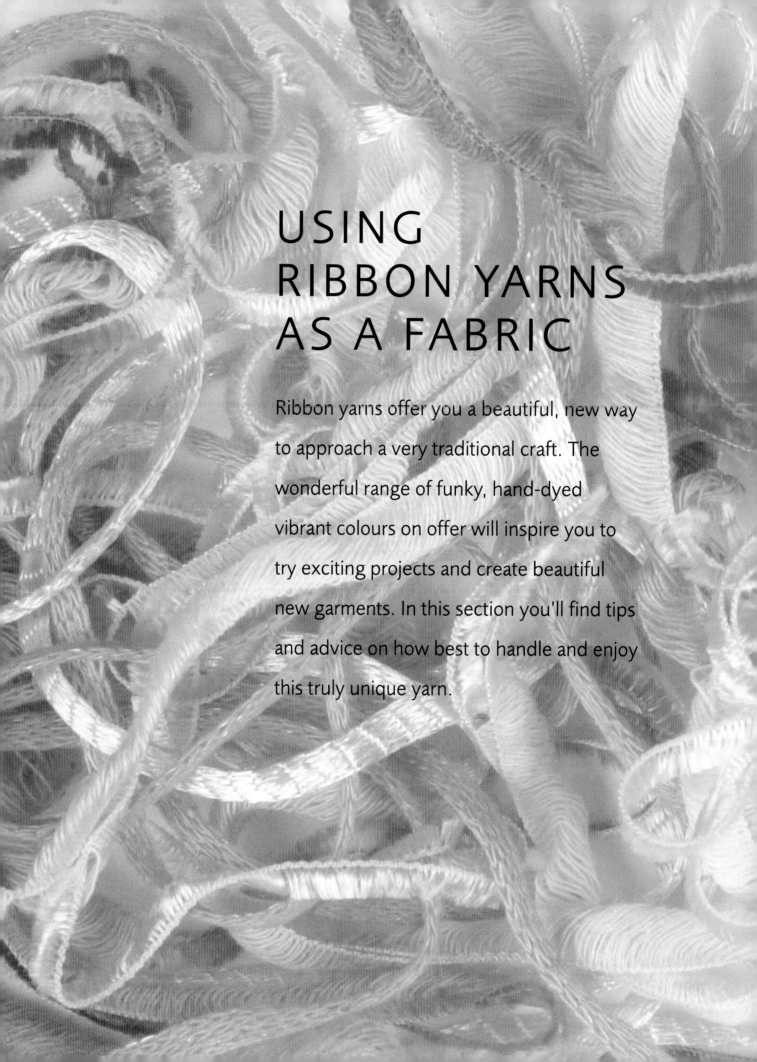

USING
RIBBON YARNS
AS A FABRIC

Ribbon yarns offer you a beautiful, new way to approach a very traditional craft. The wonderful range of funky, hand-dyed vibrant colours on offer will inspire you to try exciting projects and create beautiful new garments. In this section you'll find tips and advice on how best to handle and enjoy this truly unique yarn.

A FRESH APPROACH TO KNITTING

Ribbon yarn is a versatile medium and each range has its own special qualities. It's possible to substitute one for another, and they are available in a variety of weights, widths and textures. Ribbon yarns can be flat and silky or slubby and holey. Having such a variety of textures and colours at your fingertips will inspire you to experiment and take a fresh look at the age-old craft of knitting.

A whole new look

Experiment with different textured designs to produce new effects. Try cables with surface textures, and lace work with bobbles. Combine tried-and-tested techniques with a modern approach. Your garments will take on a whole new look. Team up ribbon knits with funky accessories, or use them to create a piece of personal, one-of-a-kind art for your home.

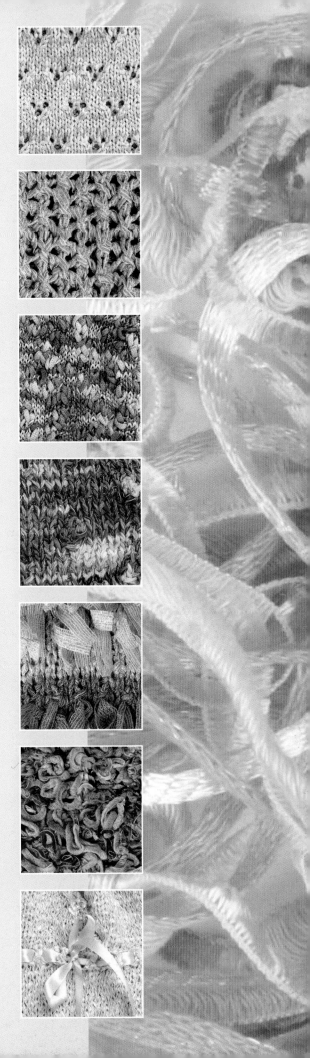

ADVICE FOR USING RIBBON YARNS

As with any new project, it's always worth planning ahead. Take a little time and read through some of the points highlighted below. Once you familiarize yourself with the unique medium of ribbon yarn, you'll be able to use it to its full advantage.

NOTE
Great care needs to be taken when knitting with ribbon. To maintain an even tension, remember to keep the ribbon flat and untangled. Other tips include removing ball bands when starting a new ball to avoid snagging, keeping an elastic band on the very silky yarns to stop them unravelling, and using stitch stoppers on the ends of your needles to avoid stitches slipping off. It is also always a good idea to store your knitting in a bag.

Reading the ball band

When buying yarn, read the information contained on the ball band. This information will include needle size and tension information (**1**), recommendations for the care of the garment (**2**), an illustration of a particular garment and how much yarn you'll need to complete it (**3**), the weight of the ball (**4**), the meterage (yardage) of the ball (**5**), the shade colour (**6**), the dye lot colour (**7**) and the fibre content (**8**). Make sure that all the ribbon is from the same batch, for even a minor variation can be quite noticeable on the garment. This is critical because many ribbon yarns are hand dyed and their look is unique. Buy all the yarn required for the garment at the same time. You may find that later on that particular dye lot may no longer be available.

Caring for yarns

Clean hand-knitted ribbon-yarn garments lightly and often, but with great care. Hand knits are not as resilient as ready to wear garments; they are more likely to stretch out of shape or shrink if handled incorrectly. There are three methods of laundering ribbon knits: hand washing, machine washing and dry cleaning. Unless symbols on the ball band specifically indicate that machine washing is possible, it is safest to hand wash, using a mild detergent formulated especially for delicates and a cool temperature.

MAKING SUBSTITUTIONS

Ribbons vary enormously in thickness and width from very fine to very bulky. The ribbons suggested for each design can be substituted, but extra care should be taken to ensure that correct tension is achieved.

When substituting one yarn for another, always check the amount of metres or yards on the ball, as the lengths often vary between yarns. This is the case even if the weight of the ball is the same. Double check the total weight of the yarn required for the design as well as the length. This way you can be sure you have enough to complete the project.

GROUP 1: Wide ribbons
The ribbons in this group are the widest. These tend to be the heavier weight yarns that produce the most 'drape'. These yarns are usually all synthetic, the majority being polyester with a fabulous sheen. Lurex might even be added to enhance their texture.

GROUP 2: Medium-width ribbons
These yarns have quite unusual appearances. At a glance, you can often tell that these ribbons have been 'printed' or 'dipped'. If one of these ribbons has a fluffy appearance, it is most likely because a small amount of Merino wool has been added during the manufacturing stage.

GROUP 3: Narrow ribbons
These fine ribbons are most suited to lacy designs and fluid sampling. They are often silky and smooth and generally have more meterage (yardage) per ball by weight. Sometimes combined with cotton, these ribbons contain more viscose than the others. This group is the most stable in terms of strength and durability.

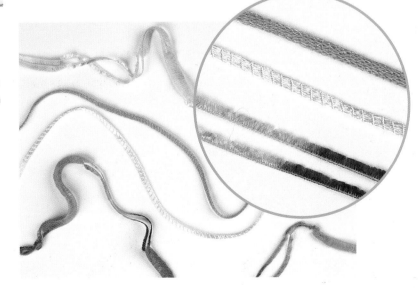

THE IMPORTANCE OF TENSION

Why do so many knitters have a blind spot when it comes to tension? The only reason that designers make such a fuss about obtaining the correct tension is that it is this figure that determines the measurements of the item you wish to create. The figures given in the tension section of a pattern tell you the number of stitches and rows required to produce a 10cm (4 inch) measurement. The needle size used to achieve this is suggested to give you an idea of the most likely needle size to work with. Knitters, however, vary enormously in the way that they work. Do not be surprised if you have to change needle sizes to achieve the correct tension.

Measuring tension

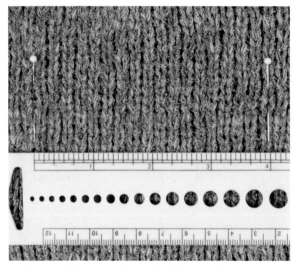

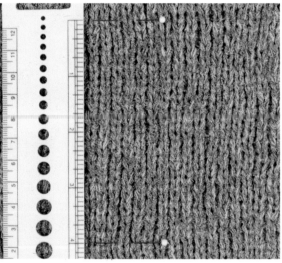

1 *Cast on sufficient stitches to be able to work a swatch/sample at least 12cm (5 in) in width. Some patterns give the tension over 12cm (5 in), however a larger sample gives a more accurate measurement. Work in the required pattern until the piece measures approximately 12cm (5 in) then break the yarn, thread it through the stitches, and measure the amount of stitches. Pin a section that measures 10cm (4 in) exactly and then count the stitches across.*

2 *Repeat the same process to measure the rows by pinning a 10cm (4 in) section vertically on the finished sample. You might find that the rows can be counted more easily on the reverse because the stitches are more defined. Any slight inaccuracies in row tension can be overlooked due to the fact that the lengthwise proportions of a garment are usually given as a meaurement.*

Too loose
The sample above looks floppy and unstable because there are too few stitches per 10cm (4 in). Use a smaller needle to achieve the correct tension.

Correct tension
The stitches are formed in a united and neat manner. Use an example that measures the same as that recommended by the designer.

Too tight
The sample looks stiff and unmanageable because there are too many stitches per 10cm (4 in). To fix, change to a bigger needle size.

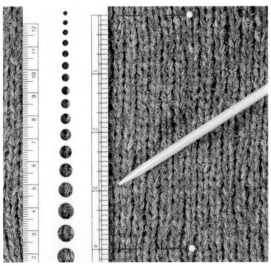

3 *You must be accurate when measuring stitch tension. Just half a stitch out over 10cm (4 in) becomes a large inaccuracy over the full width of a garment. This can result in a dramatic increase or reduction in sizing.*

If the measurement between the points is more than 10cm (4 in) then your knitting is too loose; if less, than it is too tight.

Take your time

Before learning to knit, find a comfortable, quiet space that is well lit, and relax – it should be an enjoyable experience. Make sure that the chair in which you are sitting supports your back and allows your arms to move freely. Allow yourself plenty of time to get to grips with the basics; everyone learns at a different speed, so the right pace is your pace. This would be an ideal time and opportunity to master your tension, adjust needle sizing if required, and familiarize yourself with the design itself.

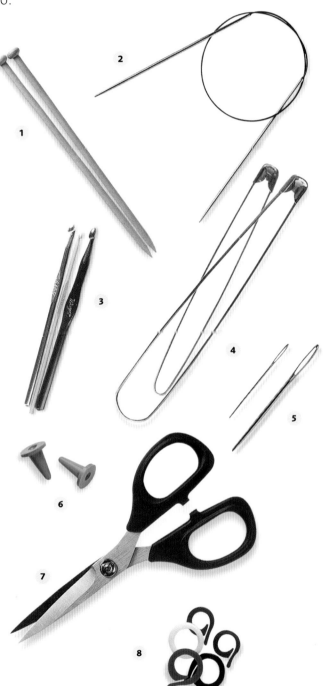

EQUIPMENT NEEDED

Your pattern will tell you what tools and equipment are required, as well as recommended needle sizes, and yarn types and amounts. Stock up on the tools listed below, also.

Some of these items are essential, some optional. You will also need a knitting bag and a notepad and pen.

1 BAMBOO NEEDLES with gentle ends are useful when knitting large, heavier ribbons. They tend not to split the ribbons, as ordinary steel needles might.

2 CIRCULAR NEEDLES Used for tubular or straight knitting when you have too many stitches to comfortably fit on regular knitting needles.

3 CROCHET HOOKS Used for working crochet edges and motifs, button loops and surface detailing.

4 STITCH HOLDERS Handy to retain stitches before constructing a garment.

5 TAPESTRY NEEDLES Used for sewing up garments and doing embroidery on knitted fabrics. They are particularly useful for ribbon work as they do not split the yarn, thereby making the construction process much easier.

6 STITCH STOPPERS Used to prevent the work slipping off the ends of the needles. Ribbon has a tendency to do this.

7 SCISSORS

8 RING MARKERS Used to mark the beginning of rounds in circular knitting and to indicate where shaping occurs in certain patterns.

9 GLASS HEADED PINS

10 BOBBINS Used for holding small amounts of yarn when working with two or more colours across a row (intarsia).

11 TAPE MEASURE An essential piece of equipment used when, for instance, measuring tension.

12 ROW COUNTERS

Equivalent needle sizes

UK	metric (mm)	USA
000	10	15
00	9	13
0	8	11
1	7.5	
2	7	
3	6.5	10½
4	6	10
5	5.5	9
6	5	8
7	4.5	7
8	4	6
9	3.75	5
	3.5	4
10	3.25	3
11	3	
12	2.75	2
	2.5	
13	2.25	1
14	2	0

Choosing beads for ribbon yarn

Although you can sew a few beads directly onto a finished piece of knitting, if a lot of bead embellishment is required, and if they are to be placed evenly over part, or all, of the design, they should be knitted in.

When choosing beads for ribbon, select ones that have a hole large enough for the ribbon to slip through easily; otherwise the ribbon is likely to become frayed or simply break altogether. It is worth paying attention to the selection of each bead. Ensure that the holes are clean and smooth to reduce the threat of snags.

Choosing buttons for ribbon yarn

There is much more flexibility when choosing buttons to use with ribbon yarns. Ribbons tend to have a unique beauty and so it is a fantastic opportunity to experiment. Use a fine needle and sewing thread to attach the buttons. Remember to choose lighter weight buttons to avoid distorting the finished garment.

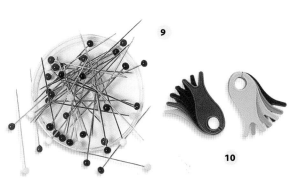

9

10

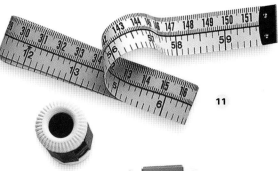

11

12

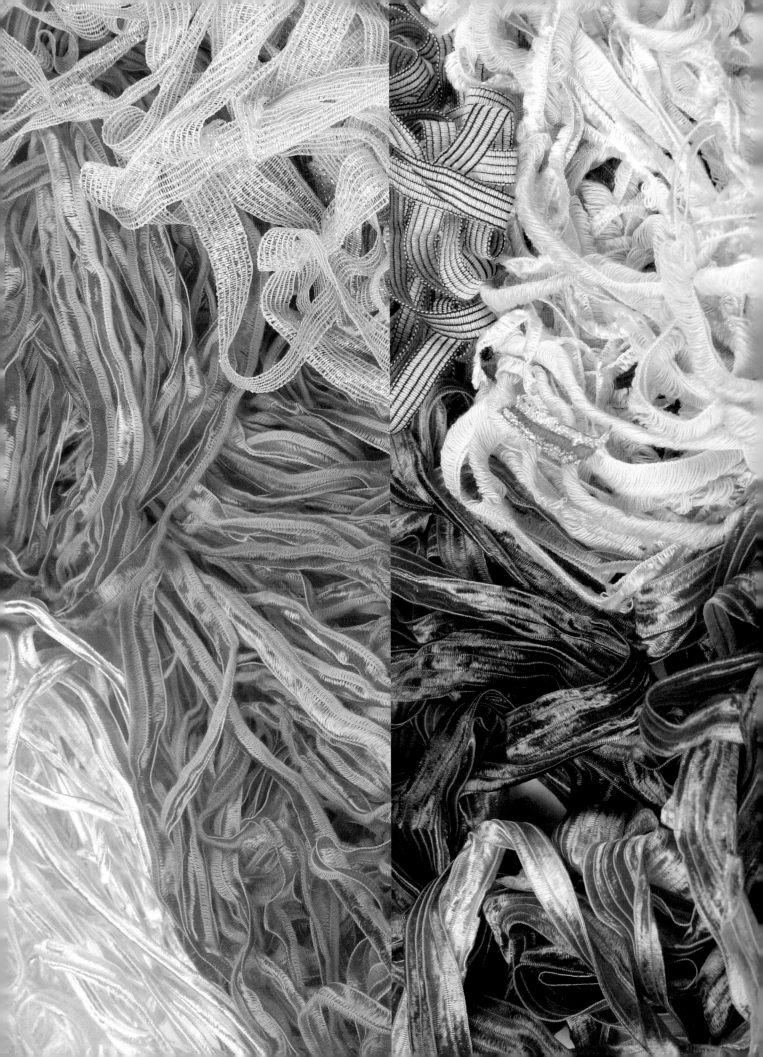

CORE TECHNIQUES

In this section, you will find enough technical advice and support to enable you to achieve professional results every time you knit with ribbon. Each topic features step-by-step illustrations and clear directions. From reading a pattern with confidence to advice on choosing a zip or lining, the following pages contain all the information you need to start knitting with ribbon yarn.

HOLDING RIBBON YARN AND CASTING ON

Before casting on, it's necessary to decide which of the numerous casting-on methods is most suitable for you and your ribbon yarn. Try each of the techniques illustrated to figure out which is best for you.

Holding the yarn

The yarn may be held either in the right hand (English method) or the left hand (European method). There are various methods of winding the yarn around the fingers to control the tension on the ribbon and so produce even knitting. In time you'll probably develop a favourite way to work with ribbon yarn, as it can be difficult to maintain continuity and very slippery.

English method

European method

Holding the needles

Hold the right needle in the same position as a pencil. For casting on and working the first few rows, the knitted piece passes between the thumb and the index finger. As the knitting grows, slide the thumb under the knitted piece, holding the needle from below.
*   The left needle is held lightly over the top. If the English method of knitting is preferred, use the thumb and index finger to control the tip. If the European method is used, control the tip using the thumb and the middle finger.*

Handling ribbon yarn

When you start working with ribbon yarns you will quickly notice that they at first seem quite unconventional. You can, however, use every stitch imaginable to obtain a totally unique look.

Needles
It's very easy to accidentally split the material with the needles, so make sure to select knitting needles with the bluntest points.

Handling
Take extra care not to overtwist the ribbon. Practise on a sample swatch to get the feel. Try running a metre (yard) or so of yarn through your fingers before you knit. This will help to keep the fabric flat as you knit, and it is a useful way to discover any flaws before you knit them into your work.

German method

1 The feed of yarn when using the German method of cast on is controlled by the left hand. This hand also supports the left-hand needle. In this method, the right hand and needle tends to be much more active during the cast-on process.

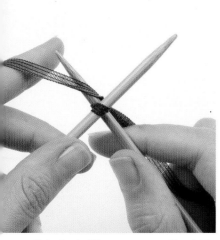

2 As the knitting progresses, the right hand supports the work as it begins to grow. The left index finger is usually placed quite high. This is a real bonus when using ribbons because it maintains a continuous feed of untwisted yarn.

Scottish method

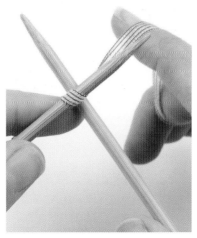

1 This traditional method is often used when the needles are supported further away from the points. The feed of yarn is operated from the right hand. The index finger keeps the ribbon flat and even.

2 The left-hand needle is usually tucked under the arm and the movement and yarn feeds are all done by the right hand. This hand also acts as a support for the right needle and the thumb is often used as a guide.

French method

1 This method of holding yarns and needles is often used by people new to knitting because it involves the stitches being further away from the points, therefore making the stitches less likely to slip off.

2 You will also notice that when the ribbons are passed around and over the left-hand needle, the right hand releases the needle, thereby enabling the support to be maintained by the knitting itself and allowing the knitter to freely operate the yarn.

Casting on

Casting on is the term used for making a row of stitches as a foundation for knitting. It is useful to know a few of the most popular ways of casting on because each method serves a different purpose according to the type of fabric you're using, or the type of edge you require. It's important for all beginners to practise their casting on until they can achieve a smooth, even edge every time.

Casting on

If casting on, for example, 100 stitches, estimate the amount of yarn you are going to need and run this length through your fingers to check for knots. This is a time- and sanity-saving technique that allows you to avoid unpleasant surprises halfway into your knitting. By doing this before you cast on, you'll maintain a tidy cast-on edge and make your knitting stronger and more secure.

1 Thumb method *Make a slip knot in the ball of yarn, a meter (yard) from the end (this length varies with the amount of stitches needed). Put this loop onto the needle as illustrated. The needle should be in your right hand with the yarn hooked around your left thumb.*

2 *Working with the short piece of yarn in your left hand, pass this around the left thumb to the palm of the hand. Insert the point of the needle into the loop on the thumb and bring forward the long end of yarn from the ball.*

3 *Wind the long end of yarn under and then over the point of the needle, and down through the loop on the thumb.*

4 *This will leave you with a newly formed stitch on your needles which you will need to tighten up. In order to do this, you must pull the short end, noting that the yarn is then wound around the thumb ready for the next stitch. Continue in this way until you have the required number of stitches.*

Cable cast-on

This method requires the use of two needles. It gives a very firm, neat finish that is ideal as a basis for ribbing or any other firm stitch.

1 *Make a slip knot near the cut end of the yarn and place it onto the left-hand needle.*

2 *Holding the yarn at the back of the needles, insert the right-hand needle upward through the slip knot from left to right and pass the yarn over the point of the right needle.*

3 *Catch the yarn with the right-hand needle and draw it back through the stitch you are already using. With the points of the needles facing the same way, slide it onto the left-hand needle and tighten up.*

4 *Release the right-hand needle from the stitch as shown and then insert the right-hand needle between the two stitches on the left-hand needle. Wind the yarn around the point of the right-hand needle.*

5 *Draw a loop through and place it on the left-hand needle as you did previously. Repeat steps 3 and 4 until you have completed the required number of stitches.*

Slip knot

You need to make a slip knot as the first step for either casting-on methods.

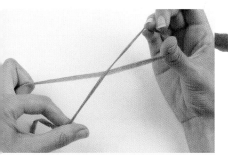

1 *Make a loop with the yarn using your fingers. The loop should be in your right hand, your left hand holding the two strands.*

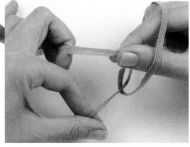

2 *Cross the yarns, ensuring that you pull through the yarn from underneath, thereby forming a link.*

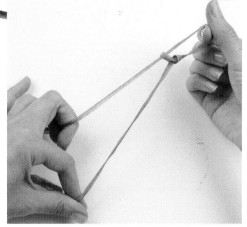

3 *While holding both ends of the yarn, tighten up the slip knot.*

KNIT AND PURL

Most knitting is based on combinations of just two basic stitches – knit stitch and purl stitch. Once you have mastered these two stitches, you can work many different stitch patterns.

Begin by casting on about 25 or 30 stitches using one of the methods on pages 20–21. Practise knit stitch until you can work it fairly smoothly, then practise purl stitch.

Knit stitch

1 Hold the needle with the stitches to be knitted in the left hand with the yarn behind the work.

2 Insert the right-hand needle into a stitch from front to back. Take the yarn over it, forming a loop.

3 Bring the needle and the new loop to the front of the work through the stitch, and slide the original stitch off the left-hand needle.

Purl stitch

1 Hold the stitches to be purled in the left hand, with the yarn at the front of the work.

2 Insert the right-hand needle through the front of the stitch, from back to front. Take the yarn over and under, forming a loop.

3 Take the needle and the new loop through the back and slide the stitch off the left-hand needle.

CREATING TEXTURES

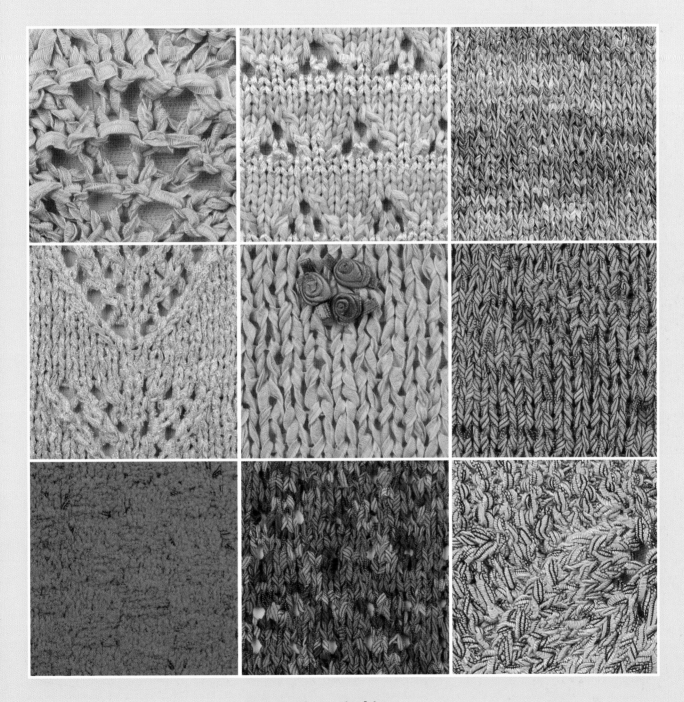

Decorative stitching

The examples above were all created by using basic knit and purl stitches. As you can see, by choosing and using a ribbon yarn with a different colour or texture, you can vary the finished appearance of any design enormously.

CASTING OFF

There is one simple and most commonly used method of securing stitches once you have finished a piece of knitting: casting off. There are various methods of achieving this, a couple of examples of which are included in this section.

Additional information

• It is important to remember that the cast-off edge should have the same amount of elasticity as the rest of the fabric.
• Always cast off in the same stitch as the pattern, unless advised otherwise.
• If your cast-off edge is tight, use a larger needle.

Cable cast-off

Cable cast-off is a neat and tidy way of securing all of the stitches so that they do not slip out of the last row worked. You achieve cable cast-off using the two needles you have been knitting with all along.

1 *At the point where you are ready to cast off, knit the first two stitches.*

2 *Slip the left-hand needle into the first stitch on the right-hand needle, and lift it over the second stitch and off the needle. Repeat this process until one stitch remains.*

3 *Break the ribbon and draw it firmly through the last stitch. If casting off on a purl row, you may prefer to purl the stitches instead, sometimes referred to as 'casting off in pattern'.*

Casting off seams together

To avoid having to use a sewing needle to join two cast-off edges, the two pieces – provided there are the same amount of stitches on each section – can be cast off together. This gives a very neat edge, and can save a lot of time. Leave stitches on a spare needle at the end instead of casting them off. Use the following method to join the pieces together.

1 *Place the knit pieces together with right sides facing.*

2 *Using the same size needle as was used in the main part of the knitting, knit together the first stitch from the front needle with the first stitch from the back needle.*

3 *Draw the stitch through the two loops as you normally would when knitting, and drop the two stitches off the left-hand needle, leaving one stitch on the right-hand needle.*

4 *Repeat step 3 until you have two stitches on your right-hand needle.*

5 *Work until you have two stitches on your right-hand needle.*

6 *Cast off the right-hand stitch of the two, as you would when casting off single stitches.*

7 *This will leave you with one stitch on your right-hand needle. Repeat all the steps from step 2 until all stitches are cast off.*

SHAPING

There are many different methods of increasing and decreasing, and they are used for many different purposes. A series of increases or decreases may be used at the edge of the knitted piece or across a row to shape it. Increases and decreases are also used decoratively (fully fashioning) and to produce many interesting stitch patterns. When used for stitch patterns, increases and decreases are usually paired, so that the number of stitches on the needle remains the same. In some lace patterns there will be a temporary increase in the number of stitches, but this will be reduced to the normal number by the end of the repeat or pattern sequence.

Decreasing at the beginning of a row

1 To decrease one stitch at the beginning of a row, it is first usual to work three stitches in pattern.

2 Slip one stitch (the fourth stitch, in this case) from the left- to the right-hand needle in a knitwise manner.

3 Prepare and knit the next stitch from the left-hand needle, as shown.

4 In this instance, you should have five stitches on your right-hand needle.

5 You can insert the left-hand needle into the slipped stitch on the right-hand needle.

6 Gently loosen the stitch and place it securely onto the left-hand needle.

7 Finally, lift the stitch up and over the knitted stitch and off the end of the right-hand needle.

Decreasing at the end of a row

1 Work to the position where you are to decrease one stitch. This should be at the same position if you are also to decrease at the beginning of the row (i.e. the fourth stitch in from either end).

2 Work two stitches together. Insert the right-hand needle into the two stitches.

3 Draw the yarn through in the conventional manner (on this occasion, through two stitches).

4 Place the knitted stitch onto the right-hand needle as above.

Picking up stitches

This technique is vital for a well-finished garment as it eliminates bulky seams.

How to pick up a stitch

Hold the knitting with the right side towards you, insert the needle under an edge stitch, take the yarn around and pull a loop through to make a stitch. When you have picked up enough stitches, remember the next row will be a wrong-side row.

Picking up along a straight edge

The secret of a satisfactory picked-up edge is to pick up the right number of stitches. When picking up from row ends, don't work into every row end or your band will flare. Skip row ends at regular intervals so that your band will lie flat. To pick up along a cast-on or cast-off edge, work into every stitch.

Picking up along a shaped edge

Don't skip stitches along the shaped edges of a neckline, but work into every decrease and row end. When picking up from a stitch pattern, space the number of stitches as necessary to fit in with the pattern.

Increasing knitwise

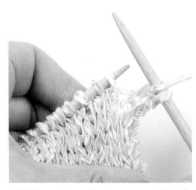

1 *Knit to where the increase stitch will be.*

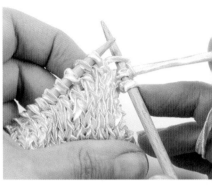

2 *With the right-hand needle, pick up the yarn that lies between the stitch just worked and the next stitch on the left-hand needle.*

3 *Place this loop onto the left-hand needle.*

4 *Knit into the back of this loop so that the new stitch is twisted. This avoids a hole being made.*

5 *The new stitch can now be placed on the right-hand needle.*

Increasing purlwise

1 *Purl to the position where you need to increase a stitch.*

2 *Keeping the yarn at the front, pick up the stitch as if you were increasing knitwise.*

3 *Using the same technique, pick up the loop in the same way and purl into it from the back again.*

4 *Form a twisted stitch.*

5 *This can now be released.*

6 *Place the stitch on the right-hand needle.*

Multiple/cable increase

1 *This technique is used when stitches are added at the beginning of a row.*

2 *Using two needles, knit the first stitch in the normal manner.*

3 *Draw the loop through the stitch.*

4 *Reverse the stitch and place it back onto the left-hand needle.*

5 *Insert the right-hand needle between the first and second stitches on the left-hand needle as shown. Draw through another loop.*

6 *Repeat steps 4 through 6 until the number of stitches required is completed.*

ADDING LINING AND ZIPS

Give your projects that professional, finished look with the right zip and a functional, elegant lining. Take your time to find the perfect match. The right finishing touches can give your gaments and accessories that extra something.

Lining

Adding a lining to a completed project can often make the item more durable and stable. The choice of fabrics is endless and the variety is enormous. Remember to take your work into the store with you when selecting a lining.

1 *It is all important to measure the amount of lining that you will need. When selecting, take the pattern repeats and design into consideration.*

2 *Always machine seams instead of hand sewing. This will make the seams considerably stronger. Allow a seam allowance, as shown.*

Choosing lining fabric

It is always a good idea to take time and browse many types of lining. The things to consider are:

Weight of fabric; will it be durable?
Colour; will it be practical?
Pattern or design; small project = small pattern repeat.

- Choose toning colours for a subtle look.
- Choose bold colours for a stark contrast.
- Combine ribbon tones with lining colours for a harmonious look.
- There's really no mystery to using colours creatively, so why not...make your project really individual.

3 *Using a matching extra-strong sewing thread and fine sewing needle, backstitch along the seams where the handles are to be placed.*

4 *Once the lining (and padding) is dropped into the project, it is ideal to turn in the selvage edges and pin it into position. Using a strong yarn, slip stitch the lining into place.*

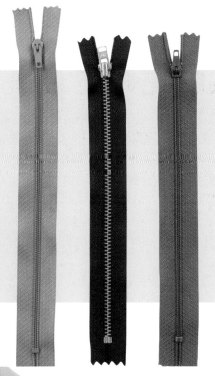

Choosing zips

Fastenings can be problematic in a ribbon-knit garment simply because the ribbon is soft and fluid and can be inclined to pull away from a zip.

Zips are available from 10cm (4 in) upwards in steps of 5cm (2 in). If you can't find a zip that exactly matches the length required, it is usually best to buy one slightly longer for a bag and slightly shorter for a garment. The one thing that is crucial when buying a zip and fitting it is that you do not stretch the knit fabric in any way during the process because this causes distortion. Do consider the colour and weight of the zip when selecting.

Inserting a zip

1 Pin the zip in position, keeping the zip teeth exposed to avoid catching the knit stitches. Fold the top ends of the zip neatly inside.

2 Tack the zip in place then, using a matching extra-strong sewing thread and fine sewing needle, backstitch along the length from the right side, close to the teeth, using small, neat stitches.

3 Slip stitch the edge of the tape in place on the wrong side to keep it flat, making sure the stitches are not visible from the right side.

CROCHET EMBELLISHMENTS

Traditionally, crochet was worked almost exclusively in very fine cotton yarn to create or embellish household items such as curtains, tablecloths or place mats. Crochet was often added as decoration or trimming on collars and fine linen handkerchiefs. Any number of adornments can be worked in ribbon yarn. With the increase in the availability of yarns and ribbons in a wide variety of textures and colours, we are no longer limited to the articles we can produce in crochet. Experiment with silky or textured yarns.

Choosing a hook

Very fine crochet hooks are usually made of steel, medium-size hooks are made of aluminium, and very large hooks may be plastic or wood to reduce their weight. The hook should have a smooth point and be light and comfortable to use. Use a steel hook with ribbon yarns as they make handling the yarn much easier.

Holding a crochet hook

For many people the most flexible way to manipulate the hook is to hold it like a pencil. Alternatively, try holding it like you would a knife. Medium-size modern crochet hooks have a flattened portion on which the size is embossed (the thumb plate), and this is the place to hold the hook in a light grip for maximum comfort and ease of movement.

Making the first loop

1 *Make a loop in the tail end of the yarn, crossing it over the ball end.*

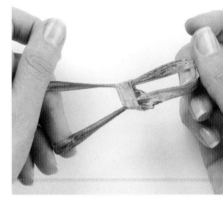

2 *Let the tail end drop behind the loop and draw up slightly to form a loose loop.*

3 *Holding the tail end and the ball end of the yarn in your left hand, pull the hook in the opposite direction, tightening the loop on the hook.*

4 *Keep pulling the yarn until the first loop forms on the hook, with a tight knot under it.*

Making a foundation chain

Stitches worked in rows usually begin with a foundation chain of a specific number of stitches. Do not count the first chain or the loop on the hook as a chain. It is always best to count the chains as you make them, then lay the work flat (without twisting) and count them again.

1 *With the slip loop on the hook (see opposite) and the yarn held taut in your left hand, grip the tail end of the yarn. To begin the chain stitch, pass the tip of the hook in front of the yarn, then under and around it.*

2 *Keeping the yarn taut, catch the yarn in the lip of the hook, and then draw it through the loop on the hook.*

3 *This completes the first chain and leaves you with a loop still on the crochet hook.*

4 *To make the next chain, pull a new loop through the loop on the hook. Keep the chain stitches slightly loose and flat, as you will be working into them on the next round.*

5 *Continue to make the number of chain stitches required.*

Working in rounds

As in knitting, crochet is often not worked in rows but in rounds. Flat geometric shapes, such as circles, squares and hexagons, begin at the centre with a small ring of chain. Each round is normally worked anti-clockwise with the right side of the work facing.

1 Make six chain stitches, then insert the hook through the first chain made.

2 Wrap the yarn around the hook in the usual way, and then draw a loop through the chain and the loop on the hook as for a slip stitch. This forms a ring of chain.

3 When working in a continuous spiral, place a marker at this point for extra accuracy.

Slip stitch

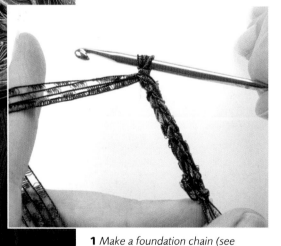

1 Make a foundation chain (see page 33). Holding the end of the chain between the thumb and the second finger of the left hand and gauging the yarn over the forefinger of the left hand, insert the tip of the hook through the second chain from the hook.

2 Catch the yarn with the hook (called 'wrap the yarn around the hook') and draw it through the chain and the loop on the hook.

3 This completes the first slip stitch and leaves one loop on the hook.

Double crochet

Double crochet is the shortest of all the crochet stitches used to make a fabric. It is a firm stitch in its own right and a component of many other stitch patterns. It can be worked in rows as well as in rounds.

1 *First make a foundation chain (see page 33). Insert the hook through the second chain from the hook. Wrap the yarn around the hook and pull a loop through the chain.*

2 *There are now two loops on the hook. Wrap the yarn around the hook and pull a loop through both of these loops in order to complete the first double crochet.*

3 *To make the next double crochet, insert the hook through the next chain, draw a loop through, and then draw a loop through both loops on the hook.*

Crochet cast-off

Using a crochet hook to cast off not only saves time, but is also useful when a loose, elastic cast-off edge is required because you can gently loosen the stitch on the hook to ensure that the elasticity is retained.

To work this method, use a similar size crochet hook to the needles (or one size larger). Treat the hook as if it were the right-hand needle.

1 *Knit or purl the first two stitches onto the crochet hook.*

2 *Pass the first stitch over the second stitch and over the end of the hook. Work another stitch. Repeat step 1.*

3 *Purl the second stitch through the first, knit or purl the next stitch.*

4 *With one stitch on your crochet hook, repeat step 1.*

5 *This process is mirrored in step 2.*

6 *Repeat steps 4–6 until you have cast off all the stitches.*

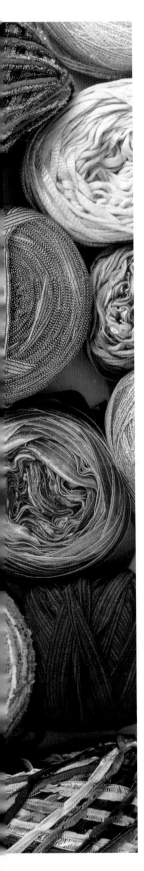

FINISHING

After many hours of knitting, it's important to spend time preparing and sewing up your design for a professional look. There are numerous ways to join seams, some of which have been included in this section, along with guidance on sewing in ends and information on those special finishing touches.

Sewing in ends

Never use a knot to join in the yarn. It is not secure enough and can look untidy on the wrong side, especially with the heavier or wider ribbons. Run the old end back along the cast-on edge using slip stitch. Never use this end to sew up.

1 Thread a knitter's sewing needle with the end of ribbon to be sewn in. Pick out stitches on reverse of the work on the corresponding row.

2 Pulling gently, feed the needle and ribbon through. Ensure that the sewn-in end doesn't distort the knitted fabric. Trim off excess ribbon yarn.

Blocking

Arrange the pieces of knitting wrong side up on a padded surface. Place pins at 2cm (³/₄ in) intervals and angle them through the knitting on the very edge of the padding (avoiding any ribbing or garter stitching). Check that the measurements are correct and that the lines of stitches are straight in both horizontal and vertical directions. Repin as necessary to achieve the correct size and shape, stretching or easing if needed.

Pressing

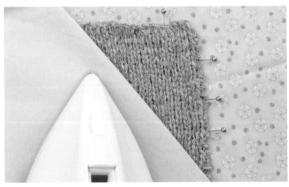

Each pinned section of knitting is lightly pressed to give a smooth finish and to help it hold its shape. The characteristics of ribbon yarns vary greatly, so it is advisable to check individual ball bands for care advice.

Cover the pinned pieces with a damp cloth and press very lightly and evenly, holding the iron above the knitting to avoid dragging the work. After pressing, remove a few pins. If the edge stays flat, take out all the pins and leave the knitting to dry out completely before removing it from the flat surface. If the edges curl when the pins are removed repin it and leave to dry with the pins in position.

Sewing seams

BACK STITCH

1 Pin the pieces with right sides together, matching pattern and row to row. Thread a blunt-ended needle with yarn.

2 Take the needle round the two edges (enclosing them with a strong double stitch) ending with yarn at the front. Insert the needle into the work just behind where the last stitch came and make a short stitch.

3 Reinsert the needle where the previous stitch ended and make a stitch twice as long. Pull the needle through.

MATTRESS STITCH

1 This seam is used by professionals and creates an invisible seam. With practice you will find that it is an easy method of obtaining a perfect finish. When starting off, leave a long end, which can be secured when the seam is complete.

2 With the right side facing you, lay the two pieces to be joined flat and edge to edge. Thread a blunt-ended needle with yarn and insert the needle between the edge stitch and the second stitch on the first row. Pass the needle under two rows, then bring it back through to the front.

3 Return to the opposite piece and, working under two rows at a time throughout, repeat this zigzag process. Always take the needle under the strands that correspond exactly to the strands on the other piece, and going into the hole that the last stitch on that side came out of, taking care not to miss any rows.

FLAT STITCH

1 Place the two pieces of knitting to be joined with right sides facing each other. Make sure that they are level.

2 Pass the needle through the edge stitch on the right-hand side and then directly across to the edge stitch on the left-hand side. Pull the yarn through.

3 Turn the needle and work through the next stitch on the left-hand side directly across to the edge stitch on the right-hand side. Pull the yarn through. Continue along the seam in this manner.

READING AND UNDERSTANDING PATTERNS

Before starting to knit any pattern always read it through; even if you are inexperienced this will give you an idea of how the garment is structured. Patterns, which are given in a range of sizes, have instructions for the smallest size printed first, followed by the other sizes in parentheses. In order to save space, abbreviations are used for many of the repetitive words and phrases that occur in the instructions.

SIZING
Garment sizes will be quoted, when applicable, to fit small, medium, and large. Measurements in centimetres (in) are also given.

MATERIALS
As well as listing how many balls you'll need of which colour yarn, this section also lists needle sizes and any extras you'll have to get.

CLASSIC SLEEVELESS SHELL TOP

The gentle wavy edge on this easy-to-knit top captures the beauty of ribbon yarns. A straightforward design with an elegant slash neck makes this an ideal project for even the novice knitter. The deceptively easy lace detailing completes the overall look. Choose a random print or textured ribbon for a totally unique garment.

Materials
9 (10, 10) x 1¾ oz (50g) balls
  Trendsetter *Checkmate* (color 1008) ribbon yarn
  70 yds (64m)
Size 11 (8mm) needles
Size 10½ (7mm) needles

Size to fit
Small 32 in (81cm)
Medium 34 in (86cm)
Large 36 in (92cm)

GAUGE
15 sts and 20 rows = 4 in (10cm) over stockinette stitch using size 10½ (7mm) needles.

How to deal with a lacy panel

1 When you start working with ribbon yarns you will quickly realize that they are unique and require specific handling. Although knitting lace is often considered "for experts only," patterns vary from simple to extremely complicated. Bearing in mind some simple tips for using ribbons (see 2), a small pattern repeat, such as this one, can be quite easy to follow.

2 Keep the yarn flat and untwisted at all times. Maintain an even gauge when putting yarn forward or back. Never overstretch the ribbon when working stitches together.

DETAIL
Actual-size detail photograph to help check tension.

TENSION
Useful tension information supplied for your reference where necessary.

NEW SKILLS PANEL
Special section designed to introduce you to a new technique you'll need for completing that particular project.

CHARTS

Each block represents one stitch. Each line represents one row. The rows are worked from right to left on the right side, and they are worked from left to right on the wrong side. Follow the key at the bottom of the chart for indications on changing colours.

FINISHED PICTURE

See how your completed product should look.

ABBREVIATIONS

beg beginning

cm centimetres

C3B cross 3 back. Slip next stitch onto cable needle and hold at back of work. Knit next two stitches from left-hand needle, then knit stitch from cable needle.

C3F cross 3 front. Slip next two stitches onto cable needle and hold at front of work. Knit next stitch from left-hand needle, then knit stitches from cable needle.

dec decrease

in inches

inc increase

k knit

k2tog knit 2 together

LH left-hand needle

m metres

MB make bobble (see page 108)

m1 make one stitch. Pick up horizontal strand of yarn lying between stitch just worked and next stitch. and knit into the back of it.

p purl

psso pass slip stitch over

rep repeat

RH right-hand needle

RS right side

sl1 slip 1 stitch from left-hand needle to right-hand needle.

tbl through back of loop

T3B twist 3 back. Slip next stitch onto cable needle and hold at back of work. Knit next two stitches from left-hand needle, then purl stitch from cable needle.

T3F twist 3 front. Slip next two stitches onto cable needle and hold at front of work. Purl next stitch from left-hand needle, then knit stitches from cable needle.

T4L twist 4 left. Slip next two stitches onto cable needle and hold at front of work. Knit one, purl one from left-hand needle, then knit stitches from cable needle.

T4R twist 4 right. Slip next two stitches onto cable needle and hold at back of work. Knit next two stitches from left-hand needle, then purl one, knit one from cable needle.

WS wrong side

yds yards

yo yarn over

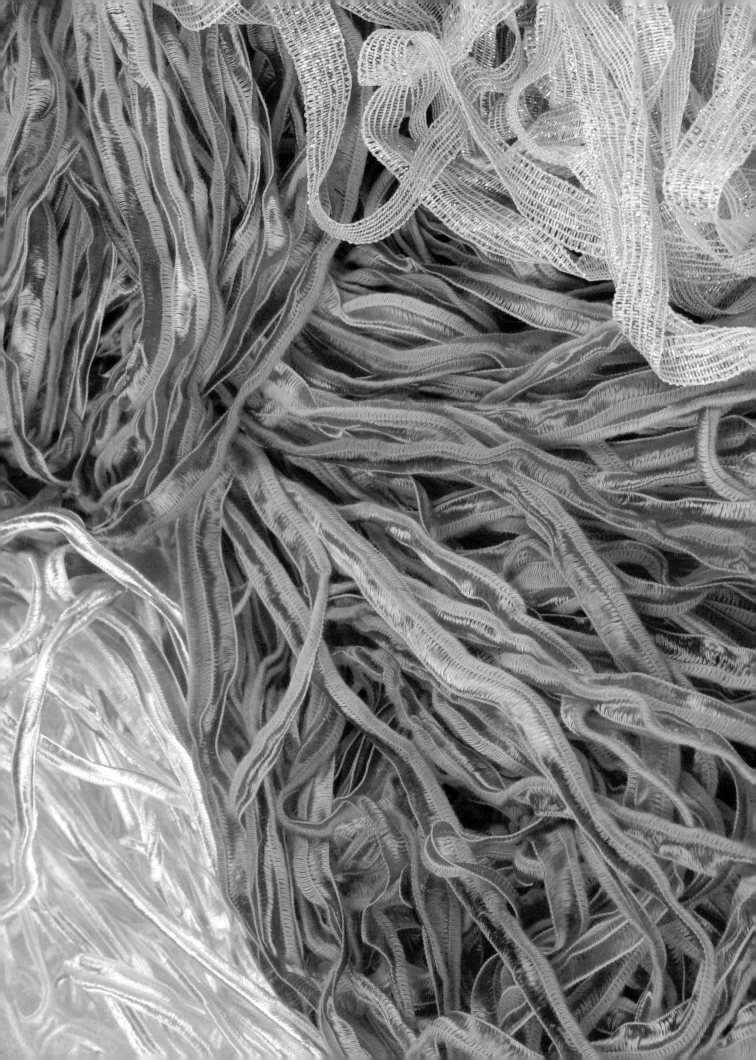

THE COLLECTION

Basic tops, delicate camisoles and summer halters, gorgeous shawls and ponchos, cozy cardigans, bright pullovers, and casual coverups— ribbon yarns add a unique twist to any wardrobe. These are pieces that are guaranteed to stand out and be noticed. The quality of the ribbons are such that you can pick and choose where to wear these items for maximum impact. They enhance your everyday basic black work staples with a real injection of shimmer, shine, and sleek color. Have a little fun. These clothes are different and special.

CLASSIC SLEEVELESS SHELL TOP

The gentle wavy edge on this easy-to-knit top captures the beauty of ribbon yarns. A straightforward design with an elegant slash neck makes this an ideal project for even the novice knitter. The deceptively easy lace detailing completes the overall look. Choose a random print or textured ribbon for a totally unique garment.

Materials

9 (10, 10) x 50g (1¾ oz) balls
Trendsetter *Checkmate* (colour 1008) ribbon yarn 64m (70 yds)
Size 0 (8mm) needles
Size 3 (7mm) needles

Size to fit

Small 81cm (32 in)
Medium 86cm (34 in)
Large 92cm (36 in)

TENSION

15 sts and 20 rows = 10cm (4 in) over stocking stitch using size 3 (7mm) needles.

How to deal with a lacy panel

1 When you start working with ribbon yarns you will quickly realize that they are unique and require specific handling. Although knitting lace is often considered 'for experts only', patterns vary from simple to extremely complicated. Bearing in mind some simple tips for using ribbons (see 2), a small pattern repeat, such as this one, can be quite easy to follow.

2 Keep the yarn flat and untwisted at all times. Maintain an even tension when putting yarn forward or back. Never overstretch the ribbon when working stitches together.

Front and back (both alike)

– With size 11 (8mm) needles, cast on 74 (92, 92) sts and knit 2 rows.
– Start lace pattern.
– **Row 1** knit.
– **Row 2** purl.
– **Row 3** k1 * (k2tog) three times, (yo, k1) six times, (k2tog) 3 times, repeat from * to last st, k1.
– **Row 4** knit.
– Repeat rows 1–4 three more times.

Small and large sizes

– **Next row** k4(0) *k2tog, k5, repeat from * to end, (last 8 sts) k2tog, k4, k2tog. [*64 (78) sts*]

Medium size

– **Next row** *k2tog, k3, k2tog, k2, repeat from * to last 2 sts, k2tog. [*71 sts*]

All sizes

– Change to size 10½ (7mm) needles and starting with a purl row, continue in stockinette stitch until work measures 15¾ (17¼, 19) in, 40 (44, 48) cm from start of stocking stitch ending with a WS row.
– **Next row** With RS facing purl.
– Work 1 row knit, then 1 row purl.
– Cast off.

Making up

– Darn in all loose ends. Join 4 (4¾, 5½) in, 10 (12, 14) cm at both shoulders using a flat stitch. Measure 7½ (8, 8½) in, 19 (20, 21) cm down from shoulder on back and front for armhole. Join the remainder of side seams with mattress stitch.

HALTER-NECK CAMISOLE WITH CROCHET FLOWER

Delight your friends with this fun and funky halter-neck garment. Beautifully designed and stylish to wear, it features classic back panels and elegant button fastenings. This camisole is the ultimate summer party top. The hand-crafted flower at the neck is a quirky touch and keeps the piece fun and light. Experiment with contrasting ribbon yarn to change the design a little and make it your own.

Materials

2 (3, 3) x 100g (3½ oz) balls
  Colinette *Giotto* **(colour 101 monet) ribbon yarn**
  144m (157 yds)
Size 7 (4.5mm) needles
4 (4, 5) buttons
Oddment of yarn for flower decoration
3.5mm crochet hook

Size to fit

Small 81cm (32 in)
Medium 86cm (34 in)
Large 92cm (36 in)

TENSION

17 sts and 24 rows = 10cm (4 in) over stocking stitch using size 7 (4.5mm) needles.

Front panel

– Cast on 68 (74, 80) sts.
– Beginning with a knit row, work 25 (28, 31) cm, 10 (11, 12) in, in stocking stitch ending with a WS row.
Shape top
– **Row 1** knit.
– **Row 2** k2, purl to the last 2 sts, k2.
– **Row 3** k2, sl1, k1, psso, knit to the last 4 sts, k2tog, k2.
– **Row 4** k2, purl to the last 2 sts, k2.
– Repeat the last 4 rows until 44 sts (for all sizes) remain.
– k4, (k3tog) four times, cast off 12 sts. Slip last stitch from RH needle to LH (k3tog) four times, k4. [*16 sts*]

– Working on 8 sts only and keeping the k2 border and shaping as before, decrease 1 st at neck edge on next and every following row to 4 sts.
– **Next row** k2tog, k2. [*3sts*]

Ties

– Continue working in stocking stitch on these 3 sts, until tie measures 30cm (12 in).
– Cast off.
– Rejoin yarn to remaining 8 sts and complete to match the first side.

Side sections

– With RS facing pick up 34 (40, 46) sts evenly along straight edge of main section. Purl 1 row.
– Continue in stocking stitch, decreasing 1 st at top edge on this and every other row to 26 (32, 38) sts *.
– Continue without further shaping until work measures 20 (22, 24) cm, 8 (8³/₄, 9¹/₂) in from pick up when slightly stretched.
– Cast off.

Second side section

– Work as for first side to * .
– Continue without further shaping until work measures 18 (20, 22) cm, 7 (8, 8³/₄) in from pick up when slightly stretched.
Buttonhole row k4 (6, 6) * yo, k2tog, k3 (4, 4) repeat from * to last 2 sts, k2.
– Continue to match first side.

Flower

– Begin with a starting chain of 30.
– Work 3dc into 4th ch from hook. * 3ch, sl st into same ch, 3ch, 3dc into (2nd ch from ch just used) i.e: miss one ch.
– Repeat from * to the end of the starting chain.
– Arrange petals and sew into flower form.

Making up

– Darn in all loose ends and sew on buttons. Attach flower to centre of front panel at the neckline.

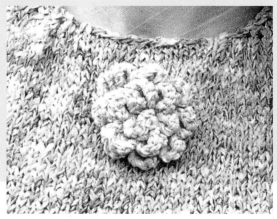

LUXURY SHAWL

This super shawl is an ideal companion to wear on late summer evenings. It's a stylish way to add extra warmth as the heat of the sun fades away. Unusual in design, this accessory has varied textures and a wealth of detailing. Tassels are an added decorative feature but are functional as well, in that they hold the shawl firmly in place.

Materials
4 x 100g (3½ oz) balls
  Colinette Chrysalis (colour 145) ribbon yarn
  80m (87 yds)
Size 0 (8mm) circular needle

Make in one piece
– Starting at lower bottom cast on 3 sts and purl 1 row.
– Commence pattern.
– **Row 1** RS (k1, yo) twice, k1. [*5 sts*]
– **Row 2** purl.
– **Row 3** k2, yo, k1, yo, k2. [*7 sts*]
– **Row 4** Increase in first st, purl to last st, increase in last st. [*9 sts*]
– **Row 5** (k1, yo) twice, k2togtbl, k1, k2tog (yo, k1) twice [*11 sts*]
– **Row 6** purl.
– **Row 7** k2, (yo, k1) twice, sl 1, k2tog, psso, (k1, yo) twice, k2. [*13 sts*]
– **Row 8** work as row 4. [*15 sts*]
– **Row 9** k1, yo * k1, yo, k2togtbl, k1, k2tog yo, repeat from * to last 2 sts, k1, yo, k1.
– **Row 10** purl.
– **Row 11** k2 * (yo, k1) twice, sl1, k2tog, psso, k1, repeat from * to last 3 sts, yo k1, yo, k2.
– **Row 12** work as row 4.
– Repeat rows 9–12 until 121 sts are on the needle ending on row 11 of pattern.
– **Next row** purl.
Divide for front panels
– With RS facing, k46, cast off centre 29 sts, k46.
– Working on first set of 46 sts only, purl to last two sts, k2.
– Commence pattern and shaping as follows keeping a k2 border on the inner neck edge.
– Pattern is worked over centre 11 sts with a background in stocking stitch.
– **Row 1** k17, p1, k1, yo, k2, sl1, k2tog, psso, k2, yo, k1, p1, k16, k2tog. [*45 sts*]

How to make tassels

1 Cut a piece of stiff card measuring the finished length of the tassel. Wrap the ribbon yarns neatly around the length of the card until the desired thickness is acheived.

2 Break the ribbon as illustrated and thread it onto a needle by the cut end, underneath the wrapped loops. Do not remove the needle at this point.

3 Tie the end of the ribbon firmly around the loops. You may need to knot this more than once to ensure the tassel will be secure.

4 Cut through the loops at the end opposite to the knot. Remove the card.

5 Wind the end of the ribbon around all the loops. You will need to wrap the ribbon tightly around the tassel a number of times.

6 Pass the needle through to the top of the tassel. This will enable you to use the ribbon to sew onto the design. Lastly, neatly trim off all the ends.

- **Row 2 and every other row** p17, k1, p9, k1, p15, k2.
- **Row 3** k17, p1, k2, yo, k1, sl1, k2tog, psso, k1, yo, k2, p1, k17.
- **Row 5** k17, p1, k3, yo, sl1, k2tog, psso, yo, k3, p1, k17.
- **Row 6** work as row 2.
- **Rows 1–6** form the pattern.
- Keeping continuity of pattern decrease 1 st at each end of next row and on every following 4th row until 37 sts, then decrease 1 st at each end of every other row to 13 sts.
- **Next row** (k2tog) three times, k1, (k2tog) three times. [*7 sts*]
- **Next row** p2tog, p3, p2tog. [*5 sts*]
- **Next row** k2tog, k1, k2tog. [*3 sts*]
- **Next row** p3.
- **Next row** sl1, k2tog, psso, and fasten off.
- Rejoin yarn to remaining stitches and complete to match first side.

Making up
- Darn in all loose ends.
- Make three tassels (see How to make tassels, page 48) by winding yarn around a piece of cardboard measuring 11cm (4¼ in). Sew one onto each of the three points made. Be sure to leave a shank between it and the shawl.

SHORT-SLEEVED RAGLAN TOP

This pretty, textured shirt would look smart enough to wear even under a business suit. Its fully fashioned shaping ensures a perfect fit. With its back fastening neatly placed at the shoulder and its cable detail adding character, the look is both classic and slightly retro. Change its identity by using alternative colours to match your personal style.

Materials
9 (10, 11) x 50g (1¾oz) balls
  Lana Grossa *Fresco* (colour 07) ribbon yarn
  93 yds (85m)
Size 8 (4mm) needles
Cable needle
12cm (5 in) zip
Stitch holder

Size to fit
Small 86cm (34 in)
Medium 91cm (36 in)
Large 96cm (38 in)

TENSION
22 sts and 31 rows = 10cm (4 in) square over stocking stitch using size 8 (4mm) needles.

Additional technique
– **MB make bobble =** knit into front, back, and front of next st, turn and purl 3, turn and knit 3, turn and purl 3, turn sl1, k2tog, psso. This completes the bobble.

Cable panel (16 row repeat)
– Worked across 19 sts.
– **Row 1** p6, T3B, k1, T3F, p6.
– **Row 2** k6, p3, k1, p3, k6.
– **Row 3** p5, C3B, p1, k1, p1, C3F, p5.
– **Row 4** k5, p2, (k1, p1) twice, k1, p2, k5.
– **Row 5** p4, T3B, (k1, p1) twice, k1, T3F, p4.
– **Row 6** k4, p3, (k1, p1) twice, k1, p3, k4.
– **Row 7** p3, C3B, (p1, k1) three times, p1, C3F, p3.
– **Row 8** k3, p2, (k1, p1) four times, k1, p2, k3.
– **Row 9** p2 , T3B, (k1, p1) four times, k1, T3F, p2.

– **Row 10** k2, p3, (k1, p1) four times, k1, p3, k2.
– **Row 11** p1, C3B, (p1,k1) five times, p1, C3F, p1.
– **Row 12** k1, p2, (k1, p1) six times, k1, p2, k1.
– **Row 13** p1, T4L, (k1, p1) four times, k1, T4R, p1.
– **Row 14** k3, p2, (k1, p1) four times, k1, p2, k3.
– **Row 15** p3, T4L, k1, p1, MB, p1, k1, T4R, p3.
– **Row 16** k7, p2, k1, p2, k7.

Front
– Cast on 95 (101, 107) sts.
– **Row 1** p2 (0, 2) *k2, p2, repeat from * to last st, k1.
– **Row 2** p1 * k2, p2, repeat from * to last 2 (0, 2) sts, k2 (0, 2).

– **Row** 3 RS, starting with a knit row, continue in stocking stitch throughout and at the same time set cable pattern in centre of front as follows: k38 (41, 44), work row 1 of cable panel (19 sts), k38 (41, 44).
– Work 13 rows.
– **Row 17** RS, decrease 1 st at each end of row. [*93 (99, 105) sts*]
– Work 5 rows without shaping.
– Repeat the last 6 rows once. [*91 (97, 103) sts*]
– **Next row** decrease 1 st at each end of row. [*89 (95, 101) sts*]
– Work 13 rows without shaping.
– **Next row** increase 1 st at each end of row. [*91 (97, 103) sts*]
– Work 5 rows without shaping.
– Repeat the last 6 rows once.
– **Next row** increase 1 st at each end of row. [*95 (101, 107) sts*]
– Continue without shaping until work measures 30 (32, 34) cm,12 (12½, 13¼) in from cast-on.

Shape armholes
– Bind off 2 (2, 3) sts at the beginning of the next 2 rows.
– **Next row** k2, sl1, k1, psso, knit to last 4 sts, k2tog, k2.
– **Next row** purl.
– Repeat the last 2 rows ** until 43 (45, 49) sts remain, ending with a WS row.

Shape neck
– **Next row** k2, sl1, k1, psso, k11 (12, 14), turn, leaving remaining sts on a stitch holder.
– Still decreasing at armhole edge as before, decrease 1 st at neck edge on next and every other row until 5 (4, 4) sts remain, working decreases on outer armhole edge when they can no longer be worked inside a border of 2 sts. Keeping neck edge straight, continue to decrease at armhole edge until 1 st remains. Fasten off.
– Slip the centre 13 (13, 13) sts onto a stitch holder.
– Rejoin yarn to remaining stitches at neck edge and complete to match first side.

Back
– Work as for front to ** omitting cable pattern.
– ** until 25 (27, 29) sts remain, ending on a WS row.
– Leave these sts on a stitch holder.

Sleeves (make two)
– Cast on 66 (70, 74) sts.
– **Row 1*** k2, p2, repeat from * to last 2 sts, k2.
– **Row 2** * k2, p2, repeat from * to last 2 sts, p2.
– **Next row** change to stocking stitch, increase 1 st each end of this and every following 4th row to 72 (76, 80) sts.

– Continue without further shaping until work measures 6 (6, 8) cm, 2½ (2½, 3) in from the beginning, ending with a WS row.

Shape top
– Cast off 2 (2, 3) sts at the beginning of the next 2 rows.
– **Next row** k2, sl1, k1, psso, knit to last 4 sts, k2tog, k2.
– **Next row** purl.
– Repeat the last 2 rows until 2 sts remain, ending with a WS row and working decreases at outer armhole edge when they can no longer be worked inside a border of 2 sts.
– Cast off.

Neckband
– Using mattress stitch, join raglan seams, leaving left back raglan seam open. With RS of work facing, pick up and knit 2 sts across top of left sleeve, 17 (18, 19) sts down left side of neck, knit across the 13 (13, 13) sts at centre front, pick up and knit 17 (18, 19) sts up right side of neck, 2 sts across top of right sleeve and knit across the 25 (27, 29) sts of back neck. [76 (80, 84) sts]
– Work 3 rows in k2, p2 rib.
– Cast off loosely in pattern.

Making up
– Darn in all loose ends.
– Using mattress stitch join side and sleeve seams. Sew zip into left back raglan seam and join the remainder using the same method.

HALTER-NECK BACK-WRAP TOP

This ultra feminine halter-neck top is all about catwalk glamour. A centre panel of elegant lace detail adds sophistication to a garment that is basically constructed in one main piece. The textural detailing on the back-wrapped panels is achieved by picking up stitches from the main section and knitting across, combining a refreshing look with an intriguing design. Although complex in appearance, this summery top is easy to create.

Materials
6 x 50g (1³⁄₄oz) balls
Lana Grossa *India* (colour 22) ribbon yarn
60m (66 yds)
Size 4 (6mm) needles

Size to fit
Small 81cm (32 in)

Front panel
– Cast on 59 sts.
– Work 46 rows in stocking stitch, setting lace panel in centre (see How to deal with a lacy panel, page 42).
Shape sides
– Cast off 3 sts at the beginning of the next two rows. [53 sts]
– Continue to decrease 1 st at each end of the next and every following 4th row to 29 sts.
– Work 1 row.
Shape neck
– k9, cast off centre 11 sts, k9.
– Working on 9 sts, continue decreasing as before on outside edge and decrease 1 st at neck edge on every row to 5 sts.
Tie
– Continue in stocking stitch on these 5 sts until tie measures 35cm (14 in).
– Cast off.
– Rejoin yarn to remaining 9 sts and reversing all shapings, work to match first side.

Side panels and ties (both sides)
– With RS facing, pick up 34 sts along side of front panel.
– Purl next row.
– Continue in stocking stitch, keeping bottom edge straight, decrease 1 st on every other row on top edge, until 5 sts remain.
– Continue on these sts until side panel or tie measures 23 in (60cm).
– Cast off.

Lace panel
– The lace panel is worked over 11 sts and is repeated every 16 rows.
– **Row 1** k1 yo, sl1, k1 psso, k5, k2tog, yo, k1.
– **Row 2** purl (and purl every alternate row).
– **Row 3** k2, yo, sl1, k1 psso, k3, k2tog, yo, k2.
– **Row 5** k3, yo, sl1, k1 psso, k1, k2tog, yo, k3.
– **Row 7** k4, yo, sl1, k2tog, psso, yo, k4.
– **Row 9** k3, k2tog, yo, k1, yo, sl1, k1 psso, k3.
– **Row 11** k2, k2tog, yo, k3, yo, sl1, k1, psso, k2.
– **Row 13** k1, k2tog, yo, k5, yo, sl1, k1, psso, k1.
– **Row 15** k2tog, yo, k7, yo, sl1, k1, psso.
– **Row 16** purl.

Finishing
– You will see from the design of the garment and how it is constructed that there is very little finishing required. The front section, including ties, is knitted in one piece. The side-wrap sections are made up of stitches that are picked up and knitted from the side of the main body, which include the wrap ties. Ensure that all of the ends are darned in securely.

DESIGNER WRAP

Completed in one whole panel, this elegant and very stylish wrap will enchant your friends. It is luxurious and drapes beautifully, and is enhanced by being totally fringed. The lacy design is worked throughout the piece and a border keeps it stable enough to wear anywhere. The ribbons come into their own in the fringe where they show off their beautiful, silky and sinuous qualities.

Materials

10 x 50g (1³/₄ oz) balls
Lana Grossa *Fresco* (colour 04) ribbon yarn
85m (93 yds)
Size 7 (4.5mm) needles
Crochet hook

Wrap

Design is worked totally in eyelet pattern with a k2 border.
– Cast on 241 sts.
– Knit 2 rows.
– **Row** 3 knit.
– **Row 4** and every other row, k2, purl to last 2 sts, k2.
– **Row 5** k2, sl1, k1, psso, knit to last 4 sts, k2tog, k2.
– **Row 7** k2, sl 1, k1, psso, * k4, yo, sl1, k1, psso, repeat from * to last 7 sts, k3, k2tog, k2.
– **Row 9** k2, sl1, k1, psso, * k1, k2tog, yo, k1, yo, sl1, k1, psso, repeat from * to last 5 sts, k1, k2tog, k2.
– **Row 11** work as row 5.
– **Row 13** work as row 5.
– **Row 15** k2, sl1, k1, psso, k3, * yo, sl1, k1, psso, k4, repeat

from * to last 8 sts, yo, sl1, k1, psso, k2, k2tog, k2.
– **Row 17** k2, sl1, k1, psso, * k2tog, yo, k1, yo, sl1, k1, psso, k1, repeat from * to last 9 sts, k2tog, yo, k1, yo, sl1, k1, psso, k2tog, k2.
– **Row 19** work as row 5.
– **Row 20** work as row 4.
– **Rows 5–20** form eyelet pattern repeat.
– Keeping pattern correct, decrease 1 st at each end as before on next and every other row until 3 sts remain.
– **Next row** sl1, k2tog, psso.
– Fasten off.

Making up

– Darn in and secure all loose ends.
– Fringing. Prepare 108 lengths of yarn each measuring 30cm (12 in), (54 for each short side). Spacing evenly, fold each length in half and draw the folded end through the edge of the knitted fabric using a crochet hook. Draw the loose ends of yarn through the loop and pull firmly to form a knot.

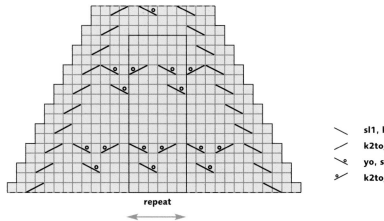

repeat

\	**sl1, k1, psso.**
/	**k2tog.**
⟋⟍	**yo, sl1, k1, psso.**
⟍⟋	**k2tog, yo.**

CLASSIC ROUND-NECK CARDIGAN

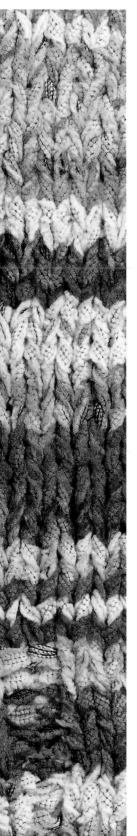

This beautiful and versatile cardigan is a must for your winter wardrobe. The main sections of the garment are worked completely in stocking stitch. Generous sizing, fully buttoned bands and a simple design with snug, ribbed neck detailing, means your winter will never feel the same again. The ribbon yarns used here create one of the softest cardigans you will ever have the pleasure of wearing.

Materials
9 (10, 11) x 50g (1³/₄ oz) balls
  Lana Grossa *Opaco Print* (colour 206) ribbon yarn
  93m (102 yds)
Size 2 (7mm) needles
Size 4 (6mm) needles
Spare needle
6 buttons

Size to fit
Small 81cm (32 in)
Medium 86cm (34 in)
Large 92cm (36 in)

TENSION
12 sts and 16 rows = 10cm (4 in) over stocking stitch using size 2 (7mm) needles.

Back
– Using size 4 (6mm) needles, cast on 55 (63, 67) sts and work in rib as follows.
– **Row 1** k0 (3,0) * p2, k3, repeat from * to last 0 (0, 2) sts, p0 (0, 2).
– **Row 2** k0 (0, 2) * p3, k2, repeat from * to last 0 (3, 0) sts, p0 (3, 0).
– **Rows 3–10** Repeat rows 1 and 2 four times.
– Change to size 10¹/₂ (7mm) needles and stocking stitch.
– Continue until work measures 28 (32, 36) cm, 11 (12¹/₂, 14) in from cast-on. Place markers each end.
– Continue until work measures 64 (68, 72) cm, 25¹/₄ (26³/₄, 28¹/₂) in ending with a WS row.

Shape shoulders

- Bind off 6 (7, 8) sts at the beginning of the next 2 rows.
- Bind off 5 (6, 7) at the beginning of the next 2 rows.
- Bind off 4 (6, 6) at the beginning of the next 2 rows.
- Leave remaining 25 sts on spare needle.

Left front

- Using size 4 (6mm) needles cast on 28 (32, 35) sts and work in rib as follows.
- **Row 1** k3 (2, 0), * p2, k3, repeat from * to end.
- **Row 2** * p3, k2, repeat from * to last 3 (2, 0) sts, p3 (2, 0).
- **Rows 3–10** repeat rows 1–2 four more times.
- Change to size 2 (7mm) needles and stocking stitch.
- Continue until work measures 28 (32, 36) cm, 11 (12½, 14) in from cast-on. Place marker at side edge.
- Continue until work measures 49 (53, 57) cm, 19¼ (21, 22½) in ending with a knit row.

Neck shaping

- **Next row** WS facing, cast off 3 sts, work to end.
- **Next row** work to last 2 sts, k2tog.
- Continue to decrease 1 st at neck edge on every row until 15 (19, 21) sts remain.
- Continue without further shaping until front measures 64 (68, 72) cm, 25¼ (26¾, 28½) in ending with a purl row.

Shoulder shaping

- Cast off 6 (7, 8) sts at the beginning of next row. Work 1 row.
- Cast off 5 (6, 7) sts at the beginning of next row. Work 1 row.
- Cast off 4 (6, 6) sts.

Right front

Work as left front, reversing all shaping.

Sleeves

- Using size 4 (6mm) needles cast on 28 sts and work 10 rows in rib as medium-size back.
- Change to size 2 (7mm) needles and stocking stitch.
- Increase 1 st at each end of the next and every following 4th row to 64 sts.
- Continue until work measures 48 (52, 56) cm, 19 (20½, 22) in.
- Cast off.

Front band (left side)

- With RS facing, and using size 4 (6mm) needles, pick up and knit 63 (68, 73) sts from front edge.
- **Row 1** * p3, k2, repeat from * to last 3 sts, p3.

- **Row 2** * k3, p2, repeat from * to last 3 sts, k3.
- **Rows 3–6** repeat rows 1–2 twice.
- **Row 7** work as row 1.
- Cast off loosely in pattern.

Front band (right side)

- Using size 4 (6mm) needles, pick up and knit 63 (68, 73) sts.
- Work 3 rows in rib as for left front band.

Buttonholes

- **Row 4** rib 3, * bind off 2 sts, rib 10 (11, 12), repeat from * to end.
- **Row 5** * rib 10 (11, 12), cast on 2 sts, repeat from * to last 3 sts, rib 3.
- Work a further 3 rows in rib.
- Cast off loosely in pattern.

Neckband

- Join shoulder seams using mattress stitch.
- With RS facing, and using size 4 (6mm) needles, pick up and knit 29 sts from right front neck, knit across 25 sts of back neck, pick up and knit 29 sts from left front neck. [*83 sts*]
- Work 3 rows in rib as for left front band.
- **Row 4** rib 4 sts, cast off 2 sts, rib to end.
- **Row 5** cast on 2 sts over buttonhole from previous row. Work a further 3 rows in rib.
- Cast off loosely in pattern.

Making up

- Darn in all loose ends. Insert sleeves at position of markers using mattress stitch. Join sleeve and side seams. Sew buttons in place.

SLEEVELESS POLO-NECK PULLOVER

Create this stunning pullover using the most basic of stitches. Gentle shaping and detailed armbands make this simple garment a true classic. Add some stripes for an unusual twist or substitute a funky, textured alternative ribbon. You might want to add a little sparkle or even try folding over the polo neck and adorning it with a vintage brooch in a complementary colour. This basic pullover would be a welcome addition to any wardrobe.

Materials
5 (7, 9) x 50g (1³/₄ oz) balls
  Trendsetter *Pepita* (colour 222) ribbon yarn
  87m (95 yds)
Size 7 (4.5mm) needles
Size 4 (6mm) needles
Stitch holders

Size to fit
Small 81cm (32 in)
Medium 91cm (36 in)
Large 101cm (40 in)

TENSION
20 sts and 28 rows = 10cm (4 in) square over stocking stitch using size 7 (4.5mm) needles.

Back
– Using size 7 (4.5mm) needles cast on 69 (79, 89) sts.
– Work 2 rows in k1, p1 rib.
– Beginning with a knit row, work 6 rows in stocking stitch.
– **Next row** increase 1 st at each end of row. [*71 (81, 91) sts*]
– Continue in stocking stitch, increasing as before on the 10th and every following 10th row to 77 (87, 97) sts.
– Continue without further shaping until work measures 25 (27, 29) cm, 10 (10¹/₂, 11¹/₂) in from beginning.
Shape armhole
– Cast off 3 (4, 5) sts at begin of the next 2 rows. [*71 (79, 87) sts*]
– **Row 3** k2, s11, k1, psso, knit to last 4 sts, k2tog, k2.
– **Row 4** k2, p2tog, purl to last 4 sts, p2tog tbl, k2.

– **Row 5** work as row 3. [*65 (73, 81) sts*]
Medium and large sizes
– Work rows 4 and 5 once (twice) more. [*69 (73) sts*]
All sizes
– K2, purl to last 2 sts, k2.
– **Next row** k2, s11, k1, psso, knit to last 4 sts, k2tog, k2.
– Repeat last 2 rows twice more. [*59 (63, 67) sts*]
– Continue without further shaping until armhole measures 19 (20, 21) cm, 7¹/₂ (8, 8¹/₄) in, ending with a WS row.
Shape shoulders
– Cast off 5 sts at beginning of the next two rows. [*49 (53, 57) sts*]

– Next row RS cast off 5 sts, knit until there are 8 (9, 10) sts on the RH needle and turn, leaving remaining stitches on a holder, working each side of neck separately.
– Cast off 4 sts at beginning of next row.
– Cast off remaining 4 (5, 6) sts.
– With RS facing rejoin yarn to remaining sts, cast off centre 23 (25,27) sts, knit to end.
– Complete to match first side, reversing shaping.

Front

– Work as given for back until 18 (18, 20) rows less have been worked than on back to start of shoulder shaping, ending with a WS row.

Shape neck
– **Next row** RS facing k21 (22, 24) sts and turn, leaving remaining stitches on a stitch holder. Work each side of neck separately.
– Decrease 1 st at neck edge on next 4 rows, then on every other row two (two, three) times, then on following 4th row. [14 (15, 16) sts]
– Work a further 5 rows without shaping. End with WS row.

Shape shoulder
– Cast off 5 sts at the beginning of next row. Work 1 row. Repeat last 2 rows.
– Cast off remaining 4 (5, 6) sts.
– With RS facing, rejoin yarn to remaining sts, cast off centre 17 (19, 19) sts, knit to end.
– Complete to match first side, reversing all shaping.

Neckband

– Join right shoulder seam by using mattress stitch.
– Using size 4 (6mm) needles and with RS facing, pick up and knit 22 (22, 25) sts down left side of neck, 17 (19, 19) sts from front, 22 (22, 25) sts up right side of neck, then 31 (33, 35) sts from back. [92 (96, 104) sts]
– **Next row** * k2, p2, repeat from * to end.
– Repeat this row until neckband measures 10cm (4 in).
– Cast off loosely in pattern.

Making up

– Darn in all loose ends. Join left shoulder seam and neckband using mattress stitch. Join side seams in the same manner.

SUPER CASUAL SINGLE-BUTTON VEST

If you've been struggling to find something delicate and versatile to wear over a dress or maybe with a pair of jeans, then this is the perfect project for you. A great vest to throw over a T-shirt for a bit of extra warmth and colour, you'll forget you're even wearing it. It's such a casual, light accessory, but it really livens up and adds a whole new look to a basic outfit. The button is meant to be big and funky, and slightly retro.

Materials
8 x 50g (1³/₄ oz) balls
  Lana Grossa *Perla* (colour 08) ribbon yarn
  65m (71 yds)
Size 2 (7mm) needles
7mm crochet hook
Large decorative button

Size to fit
Small 81cm (32 in)

Back
– Cast on 59 sts.
– **Row 1** k2 * yo, sl1, k2tog, psso, yo, k1, repeat from * to last st, k1.
– **Row 2** k1, purl to last st, k1.
– **Row 3** k1, k2tog, yo, k1* yo, sl1, k2tog, psso, yo, k1, repeat from * to last 3 sts, yo, sl1, k1, psso, k1.
– **Row 4** k1, purl to last st, k1.
– Repeat the last 4 rows until work measures 54cm (21¹/₄ in) ending with a WS row.
Shape neck and shoulders
– With RS facing, work 15 sts in pattern, casting off central 29 sts, work to end.
– **Next row** purl.
– **Next row** cast off 3 sts, work to end. [*12 sts*]
– **Next row** purl.
– Cast off remaining 12 sts.
– Rejoin yarn to remaining 15 sts. Complete to match first side.

Left front
– Cast on 33 sts.
– Keeping a k2 border throughout, work as for back until piece measures 6 rows shorter than the back, ending with a WS row.
Shape neck
– Cast off 10 sts. Work to end.
– **Next row** purl.
– **Next row** cast off 11 sts. Work to end.
– **Next row** purl.
– **Next row** cast off remaining 12 sts.

Right front
Work as for left front, reversing all shaping.

Making up
– Darn in all loose ends. Join shoulders using mattress stitch. Pick up 95 sts evenly around neck. Knit one row. Cast off.
– Join side seams using mattress stitch. Make chain for loop at top front corner of neck edge and sew on button to opposite side to correspond.

LONG-SLEEVED WRAP-FRONT SWEATER

Decorative edging on this otherwise classic sweater combines practicality with a modern feel. The wrap-front design is stylish and fresh, while basic shaping and simple constuction make this an easy project to knit up. Classic enough for smart trousers, yet casual enough to be worn with your favourite jeans, this versatile sweater will become one of your wardrobe staples. Choose a bright ribbon yarn for extra glamour and pizazz.

Materials

10 (11, 12) x 50g (1³/₄ oz) balls
  Lana Grossa *Opaco Print* **(colour 004) ribbon yarn**
  93m (102 yds)
Size 4 (6mm) needles
Size 2 (7mm) needles
Stitch holders

Size to fit (loosely)

Small 81cm (32 in)
Medium 86cm (34 in)
Large 92cm (36 in)

TENSION

12 sts and 16 rows = 10cm (4 in) over stocking stitch using size 2 (7mm) needles.

Back

– Using size 4 (6mm) needles, cast on 68 (74, 80) sts.
– Work in k1, p1 rib for 4¼ in (11cm) *.
– Change to size 2 (7mm) needles and stocking stitch. Work 8 rows.
– Increase 1 st at each end of the next and following 14th row. [72 (78, 84) sts]
– Continue without further shaping until work measures 51cm (20 in).

Shape shoulders
– Cast off 8 (9, 10) sts, k17 (19, 21), turn, k2tog, purl to end.
– Cast off 7 (9, 9) sts, knit to the last 2 sts, k2tog, turn, k2tog, purl to the end.
– Cast off 7 (7, 9) sts.
– Slip the next 22 sts onto a stitch holder.
– Rejoin yarn to remaining sts. Complete to match first side.

Front

– Work as for back to *.
– Change to size 2 (7mm) needles and stocking stitch. Work 1 row.
– **Next row** p57 (63, 69) sts, leave last 11 sts on stitch holder.
– Work right front on 57 (63, 69) sts.

– **Row 4** knit.
– **Row 5** cast off remaining 7 (7, 9) sts.
– Cast on 46 (52, 58) sts and purl across the 11 sts from the stitch holder. [57 (63, 69) sts]
– Complete to match first front.
– Slip stitch cast-on edge to top of rib on WS of front piece of body.

Sleeves

– Using size 4 (6mm) needles cast on 32 sts.
– Work in k1, p1 rib for 8cm (3¼ in).
– Change to size 2 (7mm) needles and stocking stitch. Work 4 rows.
– Increase 1 st at each end of next and every following 4th row to 54 sts.
– Continue until work measures 48 (52, 56) cm, 19 (21, 22) in.
– Cast off.

Making up

– Darn in all loose ends. Join shoulder seams using mattress stitch. Fold cast-off edge of sleeve in half. Attach to main body starting at shoulder. Join side and sleeve seams.

Frill

– Using size 4 (6mm) needles, cast on 8 sts.
– **Row 1** knit.
– **Row 2** sl1, k2, yo, k2tog, yo, sl1, k1, psso, k1.
– **Row 3** sl1, p1, (k1, p1) into yo, k2, yo, k2tog, k1. [*9 sts*]
– **Row 4** sl1, k2, yo, k2tog, k1, yo, sl1, k1, psso, k1.
– **Row 5** sl1, p1, (k1, p1) into yo, p1, k2, yo, k2tog, k1. [*10 sts*]
– **Row 6** sl1, k2, yo, k2tog, k2, yo, sl1, k1, psso, k1.
– **Row 7** sl1, p1, (k1, p1) into yo, p2, k2, yo, k2tog, k1. [*11 sts*]
– **Row 8** sl1, k2, yo, k2tog, k3, yo, sl1, k1, psso, k1.
– **Row 9** sl1, p1, (k1, p1) into yo, p3, k2, yo, k2tog, k1. [*12 sts*]
– **Row 10** sl1, k2, yo, k2tog, k1, yo, k2tog, k1, yo, sl1, k1, psso, k1.
– **Row 11** sl1, p1, (k1, p1) into yo, p4, k2, yo, k2tog, k1. [*13 sts*]
– **Row 12** sl1, k2, yo, k2tog, k8.
– **Row 13** cast off 5 sts, p3, k2, yo, k2tog, k1. [8 sts]
– Repeat rows 2–13 until frill fits around neck. Cast off. Slip stitch into place.

– Decrease 1 st at beginning of next and every other row until 22 (25, 28) sts remain, increasing on outside edge as for back.
– Continue without further shaping until work matches back to shoulder shaping, ending on a RS row.

Shape shoulders

– **Row 1** cast off 8 (9, 10) sts, work to end.
– **Row 2** knit.
– **Row 3** cast off 7 (9, 9) sts, work to end.

ULTRA FEMININE CAMISOLE TOP

This pretty, delicate halter top is a joy to knit. Choose one of the silky ribbons in the very palest of tones to enhance the camisole's feminine feel. With woven ribbon detailing on the bottom edge and an elegant adjustable band and pretty bow under the bustline, this is a stunning and very personal piece. The addition of twisted cords at the neck makes this perfect not only for a casual, evening walk on the beach, but for summertime drinks with friends on your favourite restaurant patio.

Materials
8 (9, 9) x 50g (1³⁄₄ oz) balls
  Crystal Palace *Party* **(colour 205) ribbon yarn**
  80m (87 yds)
Size 7 (4.5mm) needles
3m (4 yds), 9mm (¹⁄₂ in) ribbon

Size to fit
Small 81cm (32 in)
Medium 86cm (34 in)
Large 92cm (36 in)

TENSION
20 sts and 24 rows = 10cm (4 in) over stocking stitch using size 7 (4.5mm) needles.

Main sections (front and back alike)
– Cast on 80 (90, 100) sts.
– **Row 1** knit.
– **Row 2** k2, (yo, k2tog) to end.
– **Row 3** k1, purl to last st, k1.
– **Row 4** knit.
– Beginning with a knit row work 31 (36, 41) cm, 12¹⁄₄ (14, 16) in, in stocking stitch ending with a WS row.
– Repeat first 4 rows of pattern.
– Cast off.

Top panels (make two)
– All sizes cast on 49 sts.
– Beginning with a knit row, work 2 rows in stocking stitch.

– Keeping a k2 border on both sides, shape as follows.
– **Row 1** k2, sl1, k1, psso, k20, pick up loop before next stitch and knit into the back of it, k1, pick up loop before next stitch and knit into the back of it, k20, k2tog, k2.
– **Row 2** k2, purl to last 2 sts, k2.
– Repeat last 2 rows another seven times.

Shape top
– **Next row** k2, sl1, k1, psso, knit to last 4 sts, k2tog, k2.
– **Next row** k2, purl to last 2 sts, k2.
– Repeat last 2 rows until 5 sts remain.
– **Next row** k2, sl1, k1, psso, k1. [*4 sts*]
– **Next row** purl.
– **Next row** k2tog twice.
– Fasten off.

Straps (make two)
– Prepare six lengths of yarn measuring approx 130cm (51 in). Knot one end. Divide into three sections. Twist until work measures 35cm (14 in). Knot end securely.

How to make twisted cords

1 Cut the required number of strands, keeping the ribbon two and a half to three times the required finished length of cord. For example, four strands of ribbon 100cm (40 in) in length will produce a cord eight strands thick and 40cm (16 in) long.

2 Knot the strands together at each end making sure they are of equal length. Attach one end to a door handle and insert a knitting needle into the other. Turn the needle clockwise until the strands are tightly twisted. The tighter the ribbons are twisted, the firmer (and shorter) the cord will be. Holding the cord at the centre, use your other hand to bring both ends of the cord together, allowing the two halves to twist.

3 Keep the cord fairly straight to avoid tangling. Knot the cut ends together and trim. Decide on the finished length required, tie a knot in the folded end at the required point, and trim the excess.

Making up
– Darn in all loose ends. Join side seams by using mattress stitch. Attach top sections by mattress stitch starting at the side seams allowing any excess to be flapped across the other panel. Sew twisted straps securely into place on the top points of the panels.
– Prepare lengths of ribbon approximately 1m (just over 1 yd) each.
– Divide ribbon in half and thread into each set of holes finishing with a bow and adjusting to fit.

SUMMER PONCHO

This poncho is an indispensable accessory to anyone's wardrobe. Constructed of four panels, it is stitched together with an adjustable ribbon cord for the neckline allowing the flexibility that is the beauty of this versatile garment. The combination of stitches creates a dramatic and individual look. The rainbow tones in the ribbon yarn make each piece unique. Surprisingly, there is no shaping involved, and only very basic stitches.

Materials

13 x 50g (1³/₄ oz) balls
  Lana Grossa *India* (colour 02) ribbon yarn
  60m (66 yds)
Size 00 (9mm) needles

Panel A (make two)

Feather openwork stitch
– Cast on 52 sts.
– **Row 1** RS, k1, * k2tog, yo, k1, yo, sl1, k1, psso, repeat from * to last st, k1.
– **Row 2** purl.
– Continue until work measures 60cm (23¹/₂ in).
– Cast off.

Panel B (make two)

Garter drop stitch
– Cast on 45 sts.
– **Row 1** knit.
– **Row 2** knit.
– **Row 3** knit.

– **Row 4** knit.
– **Row 5** * k1, wind yarn around needle twice, repeat from * to end.
– **Row 6** knit to end dropping the extra loop on each st.
– Continue until work measures 60cm (23¹/₂ in).
– Cast off.

Making up

– Darn in all ends of yarn on the four sections.
– Lay out pieces face up on a clean flat surface, ensuring that the central opening is square (see diagram). Backstitch together.
– Cut a 2m (80 in) length of ribbon yarn. Fold it in half lengthwise and thread it through the opening to make a neck adjuster.

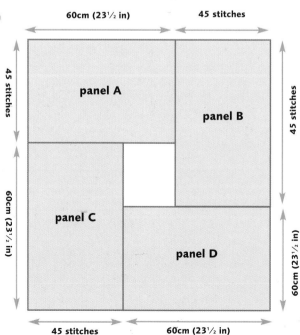

SHOULDER WRAP

This is the height of style. A beautiful gown could only be completed when teamed up with this fabulous shoulder wrap. The entire design features lace throughout and allows complete freedom of movement. The silky content of the ribbons enhances the luxurious feel and the added weight of the beaded fringe makes this a truly fantastic accessory.

Materials

10 x 50g (1³⁄₄ oz) balls
Crystal Palace *Mikado* **(colour 7297) ribbon yarn**
102m (112 yds)
Size 7 (4.5mm) needles
Approximately 108 beads for fringing
Crochet hook

– The shoulder wrap is totally knitted in open lace work.
– Cast on 79 sts and knit 2 rows.
– **Row 1** k1,* yo, sl1, k1, psso, k1, k2tog, yo, k1, repeat from * to end.
– **Row 2** and every other row, purl.
– **Row 3** k2, * yo, sl1, k2tog, psso, yo, k3, repeat from * to last 5 sts, yo, sl1, k2tog, psso, yo, k2.
– **Row 5** k1, * k2tog , yo, k1, yo, sl1, k1, psso, k1, repeat from * to end.
– **Row 7** k2tog, * yo, k3, yo, sl1, k2tog, psso, repeat from * to last 5 sts, yo, k3, yo, sl1, k1, psso.
– **Row 8** purl.
– **Rows 1–8** form pattern repeat.
– Continue in pattern until work measures 62cm (24¹⁄₂ in).
– Knit 2 rows.
– Cast off.

Making up

– Darn in and secure all loose ends.
– For fringing, prepare 54 lengths of yarn each measuring 30cm (12 in), (27 are used for each end). Spacing equally, fold the strands in half and draw the folded end through the edge of the knitted fabric using a crochet hook. Draw the loose ends of yarn through the loop, and pull up firmly to form a knot. Trim the ends to the same length and thread one bead on each thread and knot securely.

Fringing in pattern

1 In preparation, cut the required number of strands at the desired length. Thread two beads onto each strand, holding them in place with knots at the ribbons' ends.

2 Fold each strand in half (make sure the spacing between each fringe is equal). Insert a crochet hook through the edge of the work.

3 Draw the folded end of the fringe through.

4 Catch both strands securely with the crochet hook.

5 Draw both ends through the loop. Make sure they are still at an equal length.

6 Tighten up the fringe. The beads should be sitting at the knotted ends.

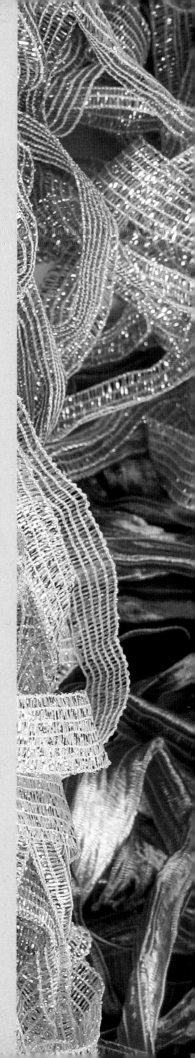

ACCESSORIES

These great projects offer some unusual places for using ribbon yarn. Imagine pulling on a pair of silky and luxurious ribbon socks after a long day at work, or a sleek ribbon yarn cap for a bit of extra warmth on an autumn day. Little touches of bright ribbon yarn accessories are fresh and fun. Use these unique yarns to your advantage and don't be afraid to experiment. Let the following projects inspire you to look at ribbon yarn in a whole new light. Ribbons can be incorporated successfully into the most unlikely of projects.

COZY SOCKS

Indulge yourself and be the ultimate couch potato in these comfy socks. Frilly and feminine, they are soft to the touch and will fit any size adult feet. The gently threaded ribbon gives the sock a sturdy construction while still feeling super silky and ultra soft. Retire from the stresses and strains of everyday life and give your feet a treat.

Materials
2 x 100g (3½ oz) balls
   Colinette *Enigma* (colour 147) ribbon yarn
   160m (175 yds)
Size 7 (4.5mm) needles
1.5m (2 yds), 9mm (½ in) pink ribbon

Sock (both alike)
– Cast on 50 sts. Work in k2, p2 rib as follows.
– **Row 1** * k2, p2, repeat from * to last 2 sts, k2.
– **Row 2** * p2, k2, repeat from * to last 2 sts, p2.
– **Rows 1 and 2** form rib.
– Continue in rib until work measures 13cm (5 in), increase 1 st at centre of last row. [*51 sts*]
– **Next row** (eyelets) k1, * yo, k2tog, repeat from * to end.
– Begin with purl row. Work 3 rows in stocking stitch.

Shape heel (first side) with RS facing.
– **Row 1** k12 turn
– **Row 2** sl1, p10, k1.
– **Row 3** k11 turn.
– **Row 4** sl1, p9, k1.
– Continue in this manner working 1 st less on the next and every other row until the row sl1, p2, k1 has been worked.
– **Row 19** k4, pick up the loop between the st just worked and the next st on the LH needle and place it on the LH needle and knit it together with the next st, turn.
– **Row 20** sl1, p3, k1.
– Continue in this manner working 1 more st on every knit row until 12 sts in total have been worked onto the RH needle, turn.
– **Next row** sl1, p10, k1.
– **Next row** k12, pick up the loop as before, knit it together with the next st, knit to end.

Shape heel (second side)
– **Row 1** k1, p11, turn.
– **Row 2** sl1, k11.
– **Row 3** k1, p10.
– **Row 4** sl1, k10.

– Continue in this manner working 1 st less on every purl row until the row sl1, k3, has been worked.
– **Next row** k1, p3, pick up the loop as before and purl it together with the next st, turn.
– **Next row** sl1, k4.
– Continue working 1 more st on every purl row until 12 sts are on the RH needle, pick up loop as before, purl it together with the next st, purl to end.
– **Next row** k12, k2togtbl, knit to the last 14 sts, k2tog, k12.
– **Next row** k1, purl to the last st, k1.
– Repeat the last 2 rows once more. [*47 sts*]
– Continue in stocking stitch until the work measures 14cm (5½ in) from last decrease.

Shape toe
– **Row 1** k8, k2tog, k2, k2togtbl, k19, k2tog, k2, k2togtbl, k8.
– **Row 2** (and every other row) k1, purl to the last st, k1.
– **Row 3** k7, k2tog k2, k2togtbl, k17, k2tog, k2, k2togtbl, k7.
– **Row 5** k6, k2tog, k2, k2togtbl, k15, k2tog, k2, k2togtbl, k6.
– **Row 7** k5, k2tog, k2, k2togtbl, k13, k2tog, k2, k2togtbl, k5.
– **Row 9** k4, k2tog, k2, k2togtbl, k11, k2tog, k2, k2togtbl, k4.
– **Row 11** k3, k2tog, k2, k2togtbl, k9, k2tog, k2, k2togtbl, k3.
– **Row 12** k1, purl to last st, k1.
– Cast off.

Making up
– Darn in all loose ends. Sew seams using mattress stitch. Divide the 9mm (½ in) ribbon in two pieces. Thread through the eyelets.

HIP BELT

Be the coolest chick in town with this sassy hip belt. Textured knitting in the main section offers an almost a woven feel. Add multcoloured flowers in your choice of tone to really make this belt your own! Stranded ties complete the project – you could even add a bead or two to make this inspirational piece totally unique.

Materials

1 x 100g (3½ oz) ball of each of the following colours:
  Trendsetter *Segue* **(colours 06, 12, 15, 1343)**
  110m (120 yds)
Size 7 (4.5mm) needles
3.5mm crochet hook

Belt

– Using colour 15 cast on 14 sts.
– **Row 1** k3 * yo, sl1, k1, psso, k2, repeat from * to last 3 sts, yo, sl1, k1, psso, k1.
– **Row 2** p3 * yo, p2tog, p2, repeat from * to last 3 sts, yo, p2tog, p1.
– **Rows 1 and 2** form the pattern
– Continue in pattern until work measures 60cm (23½ in).
– Cast off.

Flowers (make two of each colour)

– Using crochet hook and each of the 3 remaining yarn colours, make 6ch, sl st into first ch to form a ring.
– **1st round** 1ch, work 15dc into ring, sl st into first dc.
– **2nd round** (3ch, dc2tog over next 2dc, 3ch, sl st into next dc) 5 times placing last sl st into first dc of previous round.
– Fasten off leaving a 10cm (4 in) length.
– Make approx 8–10 flowers.

Making up

– Sew in loose ends of belt. Attach flowers as illustrated.
– Using colour 15, cut 12 lengths of ribbon each measuring 90cm (35½ in). Using two for each tassel, fold in half and using the crochet hook draw the strands through the shorter edges of the belt, spacing evenly. Draw the loose ends of ribbon through the loop and pull firmly to form a knot. There are three tassels for each end of the belt.

PERUVIAN HAT

This design was inspired by travels to exotic destinations. The ear flaps offer both warmth and protection and add a fashionable twist to the design. The shaping and sizing allow for a snug fit. Practise your knitting on this smaller project and choose from a whole myriad of fantastic ribbon colours. You'll soon end up with a huge collection of favourites.

Materials

2 x 100g (3¹/₂ oz) balls
  Colinette *Gioto* **(colour 102) ribbon yarn**
  144m (158 yds)
Size 7 (4.5mm) needles

TENSION

18 sts and 23 rows = 10cm (4 in) over stocking stitch using size 7 (4.5mm) needles.

Main pieces (make 2)

– Cast on 40 sts.
– Knit 2 rows.
– **Row 3** k2 * increase, k4, repeat from * to last 3 sts, increase, k2. [*48 sts*]
– **Row 4** k1, purl to the last st, k1.
– **Row 5** knit.
– Repeat the last 2 rows, seven times.
– **Row 20** k1, purl to the last st, k1.
– **Row 21** k1, sl1, k1, psso, work to the last 3 sts, sl1, k1, psso, k1. [*46 sts*]
– Work 2 rows without shaping.
– **Row 24** k1, p2togtbl, p19, p2togtbl, p19, p2togtbl, k1. [*43 sts*]
– Work 2 rows without shaping.
– **Row 27** k1, sl1, k1, psso, k18, sl1, k1, psso, k17, sl1, k1, psso, k1. [*40 sts*]
– **Row 28** k1, purl to the last st, k1.
– **Row 29** k1, sl1, k1, psso, k16 sl1, k1, psso, k16, sl1, k1, psso, k1. [*37 sts*]
– **Row 30** and every other row k1, purl to last st, k1.
– **Row 31** k1, sl1, k1, psso, knit to last 3 sts, sl1, k1, psso, k1. [35 sts]
– **Row 33** k1, sl1, k1, psso, k14, sl1, k1, psso, k13, sl1, k1, psso, k1. [*32 sts*]
– **Row 35** k1, sl1, k1, psso, knit to last 3 sts, sl1, k1, psso, k1. [*30 sts*]

- **Row 37** k1, sl1, k1, psso, k11, sl1, k1, psso, k11, sl1, k1, psso, k1. [27 sts]
- **Row 39** k1, sl1, k1, psso, knit to last 3 sts, sl1, k1, psso, k1. [25 sts]
- **Row 41** k1, sl1, k1, psso, k9, sl1, k1, psso, k8, sl1, k1, psso, k1. [22 sts]
- **Row 43** k1, sl1, k1, psso, knit to last 3 sts, sl1, k1, psso, k1. [20 sts]
- **Row 45** k1, sl1, k1, psso, k6, sl1, k1, psso, k6, sl1, k1, psso, k1, [17 sts]
- **Row 47** knit.
- **Row 49** k1, sl1, k1, psso, knit to last 3 sts, sl1, k1, psso, kl. [15 sts]
- **Row 50** k1, purl to last st, k1.
- Repeat the last 2 rows until 3 sts remain.
- Break yarn and draw through loops and secure.

Ear flaps (make two)

- Cast on 18 stitches.
- Beginning with a knit row work 6 rows in stocking stitch.
- **Row 7** decrease 1 st at each end of row. [16 sts]
- Repeat the last 7 rows until 8 sts remain.
- **Next row** (k2tog) four times. [4 sts]
- **Next row** purl.
- Cast off.

Braids (make two)

- Cut three lengths of yarn each measuring 90cm (35½ in). Fold in half and divide the six strands into three sections. Braid to 12cm (5 in) and secure. Cut off remaining yarns leaving enough to form a tassel on the end.

Making up

- Darn in all loose ends. Join the two main hat sections using mattress stitch. Attach ear flaps at the centre of each seam (on hat) again using mattress stitch. Sew on braids to end of ear flaps as illustrated.

HAT AND SCARF

Keep warm and remain stylish with this cute matching set. The hat features a novelty top with fully adjustable twisted cord detailing. Teamed with the delicately shaped scarf with its charming edging, constructed in two separate sections, it's a great winter set.

Materials

6 x 50g (13/4 oz) balls
  Trendsetter *Checkmate* **(colour 1010) ribbon yarn**
  64m (70 yds)
Size 2 (7mm) needles
Spare needle

Scarf (made in two sections)

– Cast on 33 sts and knit 2 rows.
– Start lace pattern.
– **Row 1** knit.
– **Row 2** k2, purl to last 2 sts, k2.
– **Row 3** k1 * k1, yo, k1, p3tog, k1, yo, repeat from * to last 2 sts, k2.
– **Row 4** k2, purl to last 2 sts, k2.
– **Rows 1–4** form the pattern.
– Continue in pattern until work measures 10cm (4 in) ending on row 4.
– With RS facing and keeping the k2 border, continue in stocking stitch until work measures 15cm (6 in) from cast-on ending on a WS row.

Side shaping
– Decrease 1 st at each end of next and every following 6th row to 17 sts.
– Continue without further shaping until work measures 60cm (23½ in).
– Leave sts on a spare needle.
– Make second piece to match.

Making up

Darn in all loose ends. Graft two scarf sections together.

Hat

– Cast on 69 sts and knit 2 rows.
– Work the 4-row pattern repeat for the scarf three times.

How to graft scarf sections together

1 Carefully place the pieces to be joined close together with the stitches on each piece corresponding to those opposite. Both the right sides should be facing you.

2 Begin on the right side. Bring a threaded needle up through the first stitch of the lower piece from back to front, and then through the first stitch of the upper piece from back to front. Next, bring it down through the first stitch of the lower piece from front to back, and then again through the next stitch to the left from back to front.

3 On the upper piece, pass the needle from front to back through the same stitch it came up through before, then bring it up from back to front through the next stitch to the left. If you are working with stitches still on the needles, slip them off one by one as they are secured. On the lower piece, take the needle down from front to back through the stitch it came up through previously and bring it up through the next stitch to the left from back to front, ensuring that you do not pull the grafted row too tightly.

– Continue in stocking stitch until work measures 20cm (8 in) from cast-on.

Eyelet row

– * k2, k2tog, repeat from * to last, k1.
– Beginning with a purl row work a further 5 rows in stocking stitch.
– Cast off.

Making up

– Darn in all loose ends. Join side seam using mattress stitch.
– Make twisted cord approx 40cm (16 in) long (see How to make twisted cords, page 72). Thread through eyelets, adjust to fit, and tie to secure.

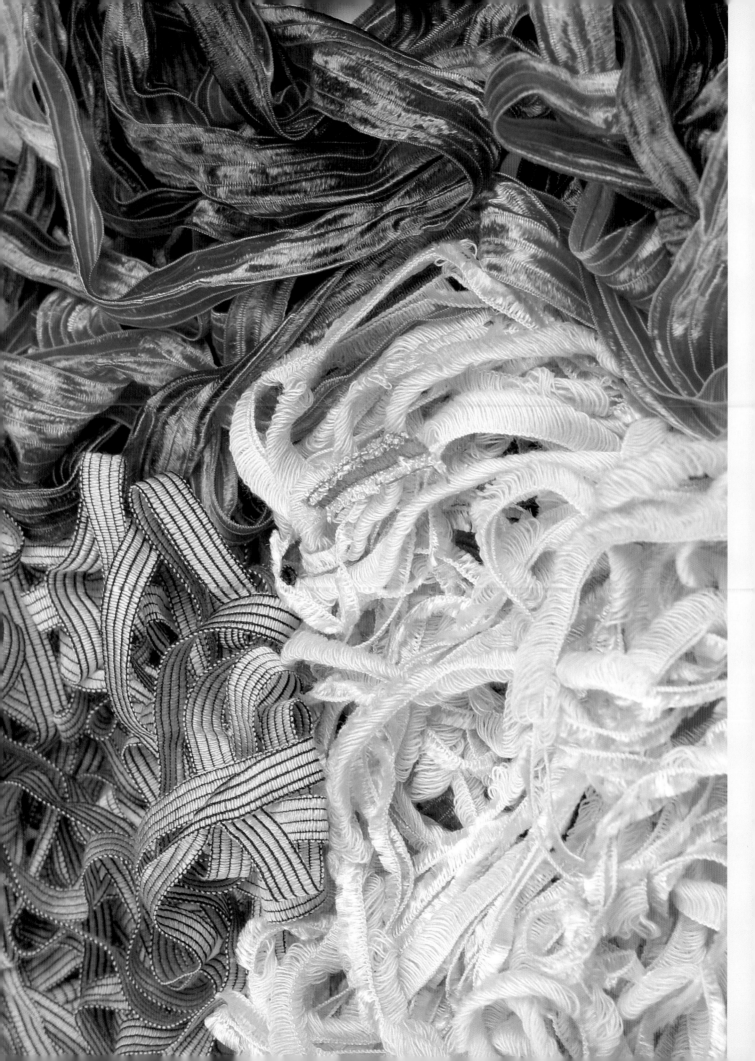

BAGS

Ribbon yarns are perfect for bags. Scan through these projects and you'll see the wide variety of bags possible with ribbon yarn. Clutches, totes, duffle bags: the list is endless. Ribbons can be shiny and delicate but, as you'll see, they can also be strong and hardy. Whether extensively beaded and decorated, practically lined, or embellished with flowers, you'll find these bags useful and convenient for your everyday use.

BEADED TOTE

Be the envy of your friends with this classy beaded bag. Only the basic stitches are used to create this design because the texture and interest is focused on the bead work. Prepare your ribbons prior to knitting and you'll be amazed how simple this interesting accessory is to complete. Glossy ribbons and shiny beads look great when used together. This is a practical bag for all your evening necessities, like your favourite lipstick or perhaps a small hairbrush.

Materials
2 x 100g (3¹/₂ oz) balls
   Trendsetter *Seque* (colour 213) ribbon yarn
   110m (120yds)
Size 7 (4.5mm) needles
Size 5 (5.5mm) needles
Spare needle
88 threading beads
6 ceramic beads

Additional technique
– **PB place bead =** place bead by yarn to front of work, slip the next stitch purlwise, place bead, yarn to back of work.

Main panel (make two)
– Thread 44 beads onto yarn before cast-on.
– Using size 7 (4.5mm) needles cast on 33 sts. Work bead pattern as follows.
– **Row 1** knit.
– **Row 2** and every other row, purl.
– **Row 3** k1, * pb, k5, repeat from * to last 2 sts, pb, k1.
– **Row 5** k2, * pb, k3, pb, k1, repeat from * to last st, k1.
– **Row 7** work as row 3.
– **Row 8** work as row 2.
– Work rows 1–8 again.
– Continue in stocking stitch until work measures 20cm (8 in) from cast-on, ending on a WS row.
– **Eyelet row** with RS facing, k3, bind off 2 sts, * k2, bind off 2 sts repeat from * to last 2 sts, k2.

– **Next row** * p2, cast on 2 sts (over cast-off sts on previous row), repeat from * to last 3 sts, p3.
– Leave sts on a spare needle.

Top edge frill
– With RS facing, join one side seam using mattress stitch. Slip both panels onto one needle. [66 sts]
– With RS facing, and using size 9 (5.5mm) needles, create fold as follows, p32, p2tog, p32. [65 sts]
– **Next row** increase once in every st. [130 sts]
– Beginning with a purl row, work 6 rows in stocking stitch.
– Cast off loosely.

Making up
– Join side and bottom seams using mattress stitch. Fold frilly top over to the RS.
– Make two twisted cords each measuring 30cm (12 in) approximately (see How to make twisted cords, page 72) and attach to each side of the bag.
– Thread lengths of yarn through eyelets and tie on ceramic beads if required.

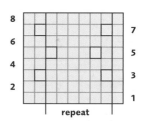

□ **PB = place bead**

TEXTURED MOSS-STITCH HANDBAG

Contemporary in styling and simple in design, this handbag is an essential accessory in any collection. The main panels are knitted in moss stitch for durability, and the lined handle adds to its stability. The whole bag is padded and lined for that touch of luxury, and zipped for security. Its clever narrow design allows the bag to be worn on the shoulder with ease. Worked in such beautiful yarns, this practical item is more than just a bag, it's a fashion statement. Deceptively easy to knit, this design uses the very simplest of shaping and stitches throughout.

Materials

11 x 50g (1³⁄₄oz) balls
  Lana Grossa *Bora Lux* **(colour 654) ribbon yarn**
  115m (126 yds)
Size 4 (6mm) needles
50cm (19 in) black lining
50cm (19 in) white 2mm padding
25cm (10 in) black zipper

Main panel (make two)

– Cast on 60 sts. Work in moss stitch throughout.
– **Next row** decrease 1 st at each end of next row. Work 10 rows.
– Repeat * to *, (decreasing 1st at each end of every 11th row) to 52 sts.
– Work 4 rows.
Divide for opening
– Work 22 sts, bind off centre 8 sts, work to end.
– Continue on 22 sts only.
– **Row 1** work 1 row.
– **Row 2** bind off 3 sts, work to end.
– Repeat the last 2 rows once more.
– **Row 5** work 1 row.
– **Row 6** bind off 3 sts, work to last 2 sts, work 2tog.
– **Row 7** work 1 row.
– **Row 8** bind off 3 sts, work to end.
– **Row 9** work 1 row.
– **Row 10** work 2 tog at beginning of row.
– Repeat the last 2 rows once more.
– Continue in this manner until last 2 sts, work 2tog.

– Fasten off.
– Rejoin yarn to remaining 22 sts. Work to match first side, reversing all shapings.

Handle

– Cast on 12 sts.
– Work in stocking stitch until handle is long enough to fit around all sides of bag panels.
– Cast off

Making up

– Sew in all the ends of yarn. Line the handle along its entire length with the black lining. This will help with the strength and stability of the finished piece.
– Ensuring the join of the handle is at the bottom of the side panels in the central position, backstitch to one of the sides. Repeat with the other side.
– Lay the partly constructed bag on its side and cut the padding slightly smaller to fit inside. Cut two pieces: one for each side.
– Repeat the process with the lining and machine the two sides together. Place the padding inside the bag and baste into place.
– Slide the lining in the very same way and place the zipper in and pin into place. Check that the zipper operates and sew securely.

OPEN-TOP ARGYLE BAG

Completed with braided leather handles for durability, this sweet little argyle bag is so versatile. It's reinforced, padded and lined to enable you to carry everything you need. Make it in colours to match your current wardrobe and personalize it by selecting a bright and robust lining fabric.

Materials

4 x 50g (1¾ oz) balls
   Crystal Palace *Deco* (colour 311) ribbon yarn: yarn A
2 x 50g (1¾ oz) balls
   Crystal Palace *Deco* (colour 111) ribbon yarn: yarn B
1 x 50g (1¾ oz) ball
   Crystal Palace *Deco* (colour 106) ribbon yarn: yarn C
   73m (80 yds)
Size 4 (6mm) needles
3m (3½ yds) leather thonging
Remnant for lining
Crochet hook

Main panel (make two)

– Using yarn A, cast on 61 sts.
– Following chart and using intarsia method complete 50 rows. Break off yarn B.
– With yarn A knit 2 rows (creating fold line).
– Work 6 rows in stocking stitch, starting with a knit row.
– Cast off.

How to change yarns (intarsia)

1 Knit to the position where the colour needs to be changed. It is important to link or twist the two ribbons at this stage, otherwise you will be creating completely separate pieces of knitting.

2 Drop the yarn you have been working with behind your work and pull up the next colour you will be using, ensuring this is twisted.

3 Keeping an even tension, continue knitting in the normal manner to the next colour change.

4 When purling, the ribbons need to be linked together in the same manner (see illustration).

Gusset

Using yarn A, cast on 18 sts.
Work 6 rows in stocking stitch.

– Knit 2 rows.
– **Next row** RS beginning with a knit row, continue in stocking stitch until gusset (after fold line), when slightly stretched, fits around three sides of panel.
– RS facing, knit 2 rows for fold line.
– Work 6 rows in stocking stitch.
– Cast off.

Making up

– Darn in all loose ends.
– Cut leather thonging in two equal lengths. Divide into three equal sections then fold each piece in half and braid, securing ends tightly.
– Using yarn C, chain stitch red detailing as illustrated on main panels. (With yarn at back of work, insert the crochet hook through the first stitch from front to back and draw through a loop, insert hook one or two stitches or rows from original point – depending on the length of stitch required – and draw through another loop, then draw this through the loop on the hook to make a chain stitch on the right side.)
– Join gusset to main pieces using mattress stitch. Attach handles securely.
– Insert lining.

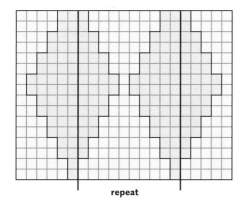

repeat

☐ **yarn A (colour 311)**
☐ **yarn B (colour 111)**

CLUTCH BAG

This is the perfect project for the novice knitter. Knitted entirely in garter stitch and without shaping, it is sure to be a success. The intructions for the integral handles are easy to follow and you'll be spoiled for choice with decorations. Add more than one flower, or select some special beads to contrast.

Materials
2 x 100g (3½ oz) balls
  Trendsetter *Segue* **(colour 02) ribbon yarn**
  110m (120 yds)
Size 5 (5.5mm) needles
Oddment of similar weight yarn for pink flower
3 beads

Bag panels (make two)
– Cast on 48 sts.
– Continue in garter stitch (every row knit) until work
   measures 17cm (6¾ in) ending on the WS.
Divide for handle
– With RS facing, k14, bind off 20 sts, knit to end. [*14 sts*]
– Working on 14 sts only, knit 2 rows. Break off yarn.
– Rejoin yarn to remaining 14 sts and knit 2 rows.
– **Next row** k14, cast on 20 sts and knit across remaining
   14 sts. [*48 sts*]
– Knit 8 rows.
– Cast off.

Flower
Using the oddment of yarn, cast on 120 sts.
– **Row 1** knit.
– **Row 2** p2tog to end. [*60 sts*]
– **Row 3** knit.
– **Row 4** purl.
– **Row 5** k2tog to end. [*30 sts*]
– **Row 6** p2tog to end. [*15 sts*]
– Break off yarn and draw through remaining 15 sts to form
   flower.

Making up
– Darn in all loose ends. Join the three sides of the two bag
   panels using a flat stitch.
– Arrange flower and attach to the top of the bag and sew
   on the beads to the centre of the flower (see photograph).

LONG-HANDLED SHOPPING BAG

Off to the shops you go with this brightly coloured shopping bag. Throw long rope handles over your shoulder and head out with the ultimate chic carry-all. The contrasting band of colour offers a light relief and added interest. Line the bag with a strong, durable fabric and get ready to 'shop 'til you drop'.

Materials
6 x 50g (1³/₄ oz) balls
  Crystal Palace *Trio* (colour 2853) ribbon yarn: main
2 x 50g (1³/₄ oz) balls
  Crystal Palace *Trio* (colour 2851) ribbon yarn: contrast
  50m (55 yds)
Size 5 (5.5mm) needles
Remnant for lining

Main pieces (make two)
– Using main yarn, cast on 56 sts.
– Work 33cm (13 in) in stocking stitch. Break yarn.
– Change to contrast yarn and knit one row.
– Change to moss stitch and work 10cm (4 in) ending with a WS row. Break yarn.
– Rejoin main yarn and change to stocking stitch.
– Continue until work measures 51cm (20 in) from cast-on edge finishing with a WS row.
– RS, purl 1 row for fold line.
– WS, starting with a purl row, work 6 rows in stocking stitch.
– Cast off.

Handles
– The handles are made up by knitting two contrasting strips and twisting them together to make a cord.
– Using main yarn, cast on 5 sts and work in stocking stitch until strip measures 100cm (39 in).
– Make another three strips to match (one in main yarn, two in contrast yarn).

Making up
– Darn in all loose ends. Join three sides of main bag sections by using mattress stitch. Slip stitch top hem into place and pin completed handles in place.
– Prepare lining and drop in. Baste in lining and then sew it in securely.

DUFFEL BAG

A duffel bag is a must-have for the gym, picnics, or a trip to the beach. It's casual yet durable and looks right at home in almost any setting. This is a very classic and traditional piece. The base, however, is constructed in a number of sections to allow you to decide how you would like the finished bag to look. Think in terms of colour combinations when you are mentally designing your finished bag. Experiment with both interesting textures and bright, bold colours to make this your own masterpiece.

Materials

8 x 50g (1³/₄ oz) balls
  Lana Grossa *Opaco Print* **(colour 203) ribbon yarn
  93m (102 yds)**
Size 8 (4mm) needles
Size 8 (4mm), 80cm (30 in) circular needle
50 x 140cm (19³/₄ x 55 in) fabric for lining (optional)
Markers

Base (work eight sections)
– Using straight needles cast on 20 sts.
– Work 3 rows in moss stitch.
– Decrease 1 st at each end of next and every following 4th row until 4 sts remain.
– **Next row** k2tog twice.
– **Next row** sl1, k1, psso.
– Fasten off.
– Join all sections using a flat seam to form the base.

Side of bag
– Using circular needle and with WS of base facing pick up 155 sts around base and place marker. Work in moss stitch rounds for 14cm (5¹/₂ in).
– Change to stocking stitch. Work in rounds (every row knit) until bag measures 34cm (13¹/₂ in) from pick-up.
– **Next row** (eyelets) starting at marker, k13 * cast off 5 sts, k26, repeat from * to last 18 sts, cast off 5 sts, k13.
– **Next row** k13 * cast on 5 sts, k26 repeat from * to last 18 sts, cast on 5 sts, k13.
– Work in knit rounds for further 4cm (1¹/₂ in). Purl 1 round to create fold.
– Complete a further 4cm (1¹/₂ in) in knit rounds.
– Cast off.

Making up
– Darn in all loose ends. Slip stitch top fold into place.
– Make twisted cord measuring approx 120cm (47 in) (see How to make twisted cords, page 72). Thread through eyelets.
– Line bag if required.

DUAL-IDENTITY BAG

Show two sides of your personality in one with this dual-identity bag. The pretty flower embellishment is sure to turn heads. You might even choose to line this bag using a fresh floral cotton print. Knitted here in the palest of pinks and decorated with magenta ribbons and striking wooden beads, try giving the design more drama by reworking it in dramatic shimmering ribbon yarns and sparkly crystals.

PINK BAG

Materials
4 x 50g (1³/₄ oz) balls
  Lana Grossa *Perla* **(colour 08) ribbon yarn**
  65m (71 yds)
Size 6 (5mm) needles
Oddments of various coloured ribbon
98 wooden beads

Main panel (both alike)
– Cast on 41 sts.
– **Row 1** knit.
– **Row 2** k1, purl to last st, k1.
– **Row 3** k2, yf, k2tog, k1 * yo, k2tog, k1 repeat from * to end.
– **Row 4** k1, purl to last st, k1.
– **Rows 1–4** complete the pattern.
– Continue until work measures 24cm (9¹/₂ in) ending with a RS row.
– Create fold.
– With WS facing, knit 1 row, then work further 4 rows in stocking stitch beginning with a purl row.
– Cast off.

Straps (both alike)
– Cast on 8 sts.
– **Row 1** knit.
– **Row 2** k1, purl to last st, k1.
– Continue until work measures 36cm (14¹/₄ in).
– Cast off.

Making up
– Darn in all loose ends.
– Prepare lengths of yarn and thread through series of holes as illustrated. Secure at ends.
– Join main panels of bag using mattress stitch and slip stitch fold into place. Sew on wooden beads and handles.

BLUE BAG

Materials

4 x 50g (1³⁄₄ oz) balls
Lana Grossa *India Cotton* (colour 209) ribbon yarn
60m (66 yds)
Size 5 (5.5mm) needles
Size 10 (3.25mm) needles
Size 10 (3.25mm) crochet hook
Oddments of Lana Grossa *Binario* (colour 021) for
flower and petals
Mirrored disc

Main panel (both alike)

– Using main yarn and size 5 (5.5mm) needles, cast on
  55 sts.
– **Row 1** RS facing knit.
– **Row 2** * k1, sl2 purlwise repeat from * to last st, k1.
– Continue until work measures 24cm (9¹⁄₂ in) ending with a
  RS row.

To create fold

– With WS facing, knit 1 row, then work a further 4 rows in
  stocking stitch beginning with a knit row.
– Cast off.

Handles (both alike)

– Using main yarn and size 5 (5.5mm) needles, cast on 6 sts.
– **Row 1** RS k1, m1, k2tog tbl, k2tog, m1, k1.
– **Row 2** k1, p4, k1.
– Repeat these 2 rows until work measures 100cm (39¹⁄₂ in).
– Cast off.

Flower

– As hip belt flowers (see page 82).

Petals (make five)

– Using size 10 (3.25mm) needles and the oddments of
  yarns, cast on 3 sts.
– **Row 1** RS facing knit.
– **Row 2** and every WS row, k1, purl to last st, k1.
– **Row 3** k1, yo, k1, yo, k1. [*5 sts*]
– **Row 5** k2, yo, k1, yo, k2. [*7 sts*]
– **Row 7** k3, yo, k1, yo, k3. [*9 sts*]
– **Row 9** k4, yo, k1, yo, k4. [*11 sts*]
– **Row 11** k5, yo, k1, yo, k5. [*13 sts*]
– **Row 13** sl1, k1, psso, knit to last 2sts, k2tog.

– Continue decreasing at each end of every WS row until
  3 sts remain.
– **Next row** sl1, k2tog, psso.
– Break yarn and secure.

Making up

– Darn in all loose ends. Join sides of bag using mattress
  stitch. Slip stitch fold into place and sew on handles.
– Place petals onto lower edge of bag and pin into place.
  Sew on securely using needle and fine thread. Add flower
  in the centre and attach. Sew on mirrored disc as
  illustrated.

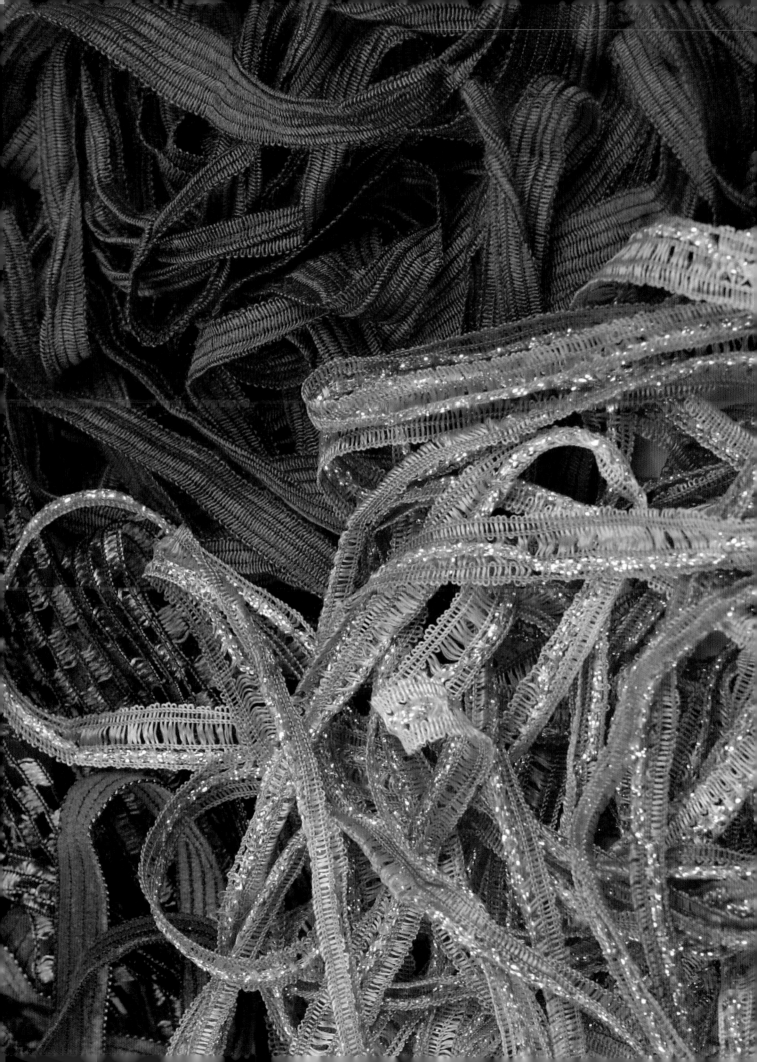

HOME

Y ou will find a selection of cushions in varying shapes and sizes in this section, each using different textures of ribbon yarns for an individual look. Subtly change the appearance of your home with the contemporary wallhanging, or update your sofas with a variety of cushions for an extra splash of colour and luxury. Select yarns that coordinate with your existing colour scheme, allowing the shades of ribbon to create new harmonies.

POPPY CUSHION

Bring a fresh spark into your interiors with a beautiful poppy cushion. With its vibrant colours and bold pattern, it's sure to attract lots of attention. While one side features an elegant poppy print, the other side is a simple crisscross print. Make a collection of these cushions for your sofa. Cushions in this pretty pattern make great gifts, too.

Materials

1 x 100g (3½ oz) ball
  Colinette *Giotto* (colour 75 moss) ribbon yarn: yarn A
1 x 100g (3½ oz) ball
  Colinette *Giotto* (colour 140 rio): yarn B
2 x 100g (3½ oz) balls
  Colinette *Giotto* (colour 141 zebra): yarn C
144m (157 yds)
Size 4 (6mm) needles
45 x 45cm (18 x 18 in) cushion pad

TENSION

18 sts and 20 rows = 10cm (4 in) square over stocking stitch using size 4 (6mm) needles.

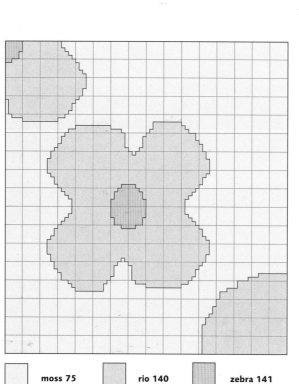

| moss 75 | rio 140 | zebra 141 |

Back

– Using yarn C, cast on 81 sts.
– Work 90 rows in stocking stitch
– Cast off.

Front

– Using yarn A cast on 81 sts.
– Working in stocking stitch and using intarsia method (see How to change yarns, page 94), work rows 1–90 from chart.
– Cast off.

Making up

– Darn in all loose ends.
– Join three sides of the cushion using mattress stitch. Insert cushion pad and close last side.
– Embroider as illustrated.

SQUARE CUSHION

This bobble-front cushion is all about touch. There's a whole series of textures just waiting to be discovered on its cute rainbow surface. Layer a few of these quirky pillows on your sofa with some single-colour cushions to create depth and interest. Create a series of these cushions using different tones and contrasting colours for use all over your home.

Materials
1 x 100g (3½ oz) ball
   Colinette *Gioto* (colour 15) ribbon yarn: yarn A
1 x 100g (3½ oz) ball
   Colinette *Gioto* (colour 139) ribbon yarn: yarn B
   144m (157 yds)
Size 5 (5.5mm) needles
40 x 40 cm (16 x 16 in) cushion pad

Additional technique
– **MB make bobble =** knit into front, back, and front of next st, turn and purl 3, turn and knit 3, turn and purl 3, turn sl1, k2tog, psso. This completes the bobble.

Front
– Using yarn A, cast on 55 sts and start bobble pattern.
– Work 4 rows in stocking stitch.
– **Row 5** k7, * MB, k9, repeat from * to last 8 sts, MB, k7.
– Work 5 rows in stocking stitch.
– **Row 11** k2, * MB, k9, repeat from * to last 3 sts, MB, k2.
– **Row 12** purl.
– Repeat these 12 rows 5 times, then first 10 rows only.
– Cast off.

Back
– Using yarn B, cast on 55 sts.
– Starting with a knit row work 82 rows in stocking stitch.
– Cast off.

Making up
– Darn in all loose ends. Join three sides of front and back panels by using mattress stitch. Insert cushion pad and close fourth side.

How to knit bobbles

1 Knit to the position of the bobble. Knit into the front, back, front, back, and front again of the next stitch and then slip the stitch from the left-hand needle so that the five new stitches are now on the right-hand needle as well

2 Turn the work so that the wrong side is facing and purl accross the five bobble stitches. Turn the work again and knit them. Repeat the last two rows once more, thereby making four rows of stocking stitch over the bobble stitch.

3 With the right side facing and using the left-hand needle point, pass the second, third, fourth and fifth bobble stitches (in order) over the first stitch and off the needle. One stitch remains and you can continue to work the remainder of the row as required.

Reverse side of cushion

FLOOR CUSHION

The hard geometry of this rectangular cushion is softened by the panelled details of frothy loops. Choose any kind of colour scheme but remember that this cushion is perfect for a clash of bright, glittery colours because of the design's fun mix of textures. Each of the sections is knitted in as the project takes shape. This oversize pillow is a comfort to have around the house.

Materials

6 x 50g (1¾ oz) balls
  Crystal Palace *Deco Stardust* (colour 4002): yarn A
1 x 50g (1¾ oz) ball
  Crystal Palace *Deco Stardust* (colour 4441): yarn B
1 x 50g (1¾ oz) ball
  Crystal Palace *Deco Stardust* (colour 4004): yarn C
1 x 50g (1¾ oz) ball
  Crystal Palace *Deco Stardust* (colour 4001): yarn D
  109m (119 yds)
Size 4 (6mm) needles
56 x 56cm (22 x 22 in) cushion pad

Additional Technique

– **ML make loop =** loop stitch (see How to knit loop stitch, at right).

Back

– Using yarn A, cast on 100 sts and work 56cm (22 in) (112 rows) in stocking stitch.
– Cast off.

Front

– Using yarn A, cast on 100 sts and work 9cm (3½ in) (18 rows) in stocking stitch ending on a WS.
– With RS facing and using the intarsia method (see How to change yarns, page 94) continue as follows.
– **Row 19** using yarn A, k19, join in yarn B, *ML, k1, repeat from * 13 times. [*28 sts*] Join in yarn A, k10, join in yarn B, *ML, k1, repeat from * 13 times. [*28 sts*] Join in yarn A, k19.
– **Row 20** keeping colour sequence as previous row, purl to the end.

How to knit loop stitch

1 On the right side of the work, knit to the position of the loop. Knit the next stitch but do not allow the loop to drop off the left-hand needle.

2 Bring the yarn to the front of the work between the two needles and wind the ribbon around your thumb. Take the ribbon to the back again between the needles.

3 Knit into the same stitch remaining on the left-hand needle, thereby making two stitches from the original one. To complete the stitch, slip both of these stitches onto the left-hand needle and knit them together through the back of the loop.

– Repeat last 2 rows another 9 times.
– **Rows 39–46** continue with yarn A only, work in stocking stitch.
– **Row 47** as row 19, substituting yarn C for yarn B.
– **Row 48** as row 20.
  Repeat last 2 rows another 9 times.
  Rows 67–74 work as rows 39–46.
– **Row 75** work as row 19, substituting yarn D for yarn B.
– **Row 76** work as row 20.

– Repeat last 2 rows another 9 times.
– **Rows 95–112** using yarn A, work in stocking stitch.
– Cast off.

Making up

Darn in all loose ends. Using mattress stitch, join three of the four sides of the cushion. Insert cushion pad and close the fourth side using the same method.

WALL HANGING

Who says knitting doesn't belong on the wall? This is as much a piece of unique art as is an oil painting or watercolour. Glossy, silky ribbon yarns abounding in gorgeous colour are well suited to this project. Ceramic beading contrasts fantastically with the wiry texture of the looped and textured ribbon surface. The splashes of colour are vivid and invigorating. Break all the rules and create as many variations on this theme as you please.

Materials

4 x 50g (1³/₄ oz) balls
  Lana Grossa *Twin Print* (colour 619) ribbon yarn
  65m (71 yds)
Size 2 (7mm) needles
65 x 45cm (25¹/₂ x 17³/₄ in) padding (2mm)
65 x 45cm (25¹/₂ x 17³/₄ in) backing fabric
3.5mm crochet hook
20 ceramic beads for tassels

– FINISHED SIZE 60 x 40cm (23¹/₂ x 15 ³/₄ in).
– NOTE that the wall hanging is worked from side to side.
– ML (see instructions page 110).

TENSION

11¹/₂ sts and 16 rows = 10cm (4 in) square over stocking stitch using size 2 (7mm) needles.

– Cast on 69 sts.
– Work 6 rows in stocking stitch.
– Continue in pattern as follows.
– **Row 1** k1, * ML, k1, repeat from * to end.
– **Row 2** purl.
– **Rows 1 and 2** form the pattern.
– Continue until work measures 19cm (7¹/₂ in).
– Work row 1 of pattern followed by 5 rows of stocking
  stitch beginning with a purl row.
– Repeat the last 6 rows until work measures 12¹/₄ in (31cm)
  from cast-on.
– Work row 1 of pattern once more.
– Beginning with a purl row, continue in stocking stitch until
  work measures 40cm (15³/₄ in) from cast-on.
– Cast off.

Making up

– Darn in all loose ends.
– Lay work out on a flat surface with the wrong side facing.
  Cut padding fabric to size. The backing fabric should be
  cut with a 2cm (³/₄ in) selvage. Tack the backing fabric into
  place, ensuring that you tuck the padding in neatly,
  sandwiching it securely. Tack and sew into place.
– Cut 20 strands of yarn measuring 25cm (10 in) and fold in
  half. Thread on a bead and knot into place. Using a
  crochet hook, attach the strands along the bottom edge of
  the wall hanging using a slip knot.

Hanging suggestions

Now that you've created your art, you'll want to show it off right away. There are many ways to display your ribbon yarn art but the following examples represent some of the easiest and most effective methods.

• **Metal hoops** Sew securely into the top corners of the wall hanging and apply to the wall ensuring the piece is tensioned to avoid sagging.

• **Picture hooks** Used in the same way as metal hoops, these hooks make displaying your work easy.

• **Dowel rod** Sew the dowel rod onto the top edge of the wall hanging. The rod will then rest easily on pre-existing wall hooks.

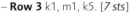

RIBBON EMBELLISHMENTS

Any embellishment created from ribbon can have a tremendous impact on the overall look of a completed project. The collective qualities and characteristics of these beautiful yarns lend themselves to be used for fine adornments, decorating and offering relief at the same time. The very simplest of designs can be enhanced with a vibrant ribbon accessory resulting in a unique and creative piece.

FLOWER CORSAGES

A corsage is a small bouquet of fresh flowers that women pin to the lapel of their jacket.

RIBBON ROSES

This embellishment is constructed in a single length of knitting that starts in the centre of the flower. As you work through the pattern, you'll see that the petals get larger and larger to wrap in upon themselves and form the corsage.

1st petal
– Using any oddment of contrasting ribbon yarn, and appropriate size needles (see ball band), cast on 6 sts and work 2 rows in stocking stitch beginning with a knit row.

– **Row 3** k1, m1, k5. [*7 sts*]
– **Rows 4–6** work in stocking stitch beginning with a purl row.
– **Row 7** k1, k2tog, k4.
– **Row 8** purl.
– **Row 9** cast off 4 sts, knit to end. [*2 sts*]
– **Row 10** purl.

2nd petal
– **Row 11** cast on 4 sts and knit to end. [*6 sts*]
– **Row 12** purl.
– **Row 13** k1, m1, knit to end.
– **Rows 14–15** work as rows 12–13. [*8 sts*]
– **Row 16** purl.
– **Row 17** k1, k2tog, knit to end.
– **Rows 18–19** work as rows 16–17. [*6 sts*]
– **Row 20** purl.
– **Row 21** cast off 4 sts, knit to end. [*2 sts*]
– **Row 22** purl.

3rd petal
– **Rows 23–34** work as rows 11–22. [*6 sts*]

4th petal
– **Row 35** cast on 5 sts and knit to end. [*7 sts*]
– **Row 36** purl.
– **Row 37** k1, m1, knit to end.
– **Rows 38–39** work as rows 36–37. [*9 sts*]
– **Rows 40–42** work in stocking stitch, starting with a purl row.
– **Row 43** k1, k2tog, knit to end.
– **Row 44** purl.
– **Rows 45–46** work as rows 43–44. [*7 sts*]
– **Row 47** cast off 4 sts, knit to end. [*3 sts*]
– **Row 48** purl.

5th petal
Row 49 cast on 1 sts and knit to end [7 sts]
Rows 50–62 work as rows 36–48.

6th petal
– **Row 63** cast on 5 sts and knit to end. [8 sts]
– **Row 64** purl.
– **Row 65** k1, m1, knit to end.
– **Rows 66–67** work as rows 64–65. [11 sts]
– **Rows 68–70** work in stocking stitch, starting with a purl row.
– **Row 71** k1, k2tog, knit to end.
– **Row 72** purl.
– **Rows 73–74** work as rows 71–72. [8 sts]
– Cast off.

To make up
Begin with the smallest petal (cast-on end) and roll it tightly into a coil. The top edges of each petal curl over to form a flower. Arrange and sew each form into place.

Leaves
Use any oddment or yarn for the leaves. Follow instructions for the petals in the blue bag pattern (see page 103). Darn in loose ends and sew into place on the base and sides of the flower.

Alternative embellishments
If you are using one of the finer ribbon yarns, you might like to thread some beads onto the yarn before cast-on in order to decorate the petals. Another idea is to sew small, clear glass beads onto the petals or leaves to represent raindrops.

RIBBON PANSIES
For this corsage, the petals are joined at the tops and bottom of each point before you move on to work on the next one.

– Using any oddment of ribbon yarn, and appropriate size needles (see ball band), cast on 1 st.
– **Row 1** k1, p1, k1 into st. [3 sts]
– **Row 2** k3.
– **Row 3** k2, increase. [4 sts]
– **Row 4** k4.
– **Row 5** k3, increase. [5 sts]
– **Rows 6–9** k5.
– **Row 10** cast off 1 st, knit to end. [4 sts]

Corsages are some of the most useful embellishments around. They are perfectly at home whether on a smart jacket or a casual bag.

– **Row 11** k4.
– **Row 12** cast off 1 st, knit to end. [3 sts]
– **Row 13** k3.
– **Row 14** cast off 1 st, knit to end. [2 sts]
– **Row 15** k2, slip first st over 2nd st.
– **Row 16** using RH needle insert point into 1st row of petal and knit it together with the stitch on the LH needle.
– **Rows 2–16** repeat rows 2–16 another four times, joining each petal in the same way.
– Fasten off.

To make up

Join all petals into a flower shape and secure.

Alternative embellishments

Conceivably, this design could be worked with more than five petals for a 3-D effect. Another fun idea is to sew some beads onto a sequin which is backed by a small circle of felt, and sew this into the centre of the flower. This look can be very attractive and effective when worked in groups.

SHOW THEM OFF

Ribbon roses

This design is large and a little heavy and it's nicely suited to a stiff, structured outer jacket. Place a three-dimensional rose on the shoulder of a jacket where a fresh corsage would traditionally be pinned. Use it on top of a pocket or to dress up a handbag.

Ribbon pansies

This five-petalled corsage is well suited to shawl or scarf ends because it adds some weight while lending the garment some lovely colour and detail. Try sewing these flowers on bag panels or on a sleeve edge.

TASSELS

Tassels are tufts of loosely hanging threads or cords, secured at the top and used as decorations on various items. The examples included here are constructed very differently and could be used on cushions, garments, bags or shawls.

STRANDED TASSEL

This design is made using a wide, plain ribbon yarn. Detailing can be added with the use of beads. The beads applied to the first stranded tassel (shown above) are made of dyed wood. Wooden beads are ideal to use with stranded tassels because they are very light in weight.

– Cut a rectangle of stiff card as wide as the required length of the finished tassel. Wind the ribbon around the card until the thickness of the tassel is reached. Break the yarn, leaving an end for finishing. Thread the end through a sewing needle and pass it under the loops. At this stage do not remove the card.

– Tie the end of the yarn firmly around all the loops, remove the card and cut through the loops at the opposite end of the knot (do not remove the 'finishing' thread).

– Wind the 'finishing' thread around all the loops below the fold and fasten securely. Pass this thread through to the top of the tassel and use this to attach the tassel to your finished design. Trim the ends of the loops neatly.

SHOW THEM OFF

Stranded tassels

These tassels become very decorative when made up in silky ribbons and adorned with beautiful bead work. They are ideal to use on cushion covers, shawl ends, or on the edges of bags.

Knitted tassels

This is just the accessory you have been looking for to adorn the zipper on any handbag. It serves as a practical "pull" to open the bag as well as adding a little extra interest. You might even tailor this type of tassel for a dramatic wall hanging or the finishing touches for a favorite hat.

How to add beads

When selecting beads to use for tassels, it is advisable to sew them on with a strong cotton thread. Apply them onto a sequin or circle of felt to act as a base. It can be easy for them to slip behind the knitted fabric if they haven't been knitted in. Figure out how many beads you'll need by measuring the diameter of the tassel and the width of the bead. It is always safer to buy one or two extra beads, just in case.

Alternative embellishments

Mix and match various beads to decorate this tassel. Try seed beads in clusters, or long, tubular bugle beads, or drops. Go in a whole new direction and use some basic embroidery stitches like French knots or bullions.

KNITTED TASSEL

This design is constructed using basic techniques. Dropping stitches off the end of the needle creates the loop detailing. This technique can take on a new look with the use of different textures of ribbon yarns.

- Using oddments of ribbon yarn, and appropriate size needles (see ball band), cast on 37 sts using the cable method.
- **Row 1** (RS) k1 tbl, * p2, k1tbl, repeat from * to end.
- **Row 2** p1, * k1 tbl, k1, p1, repeat from * to end.
- These two rows form the pattern. Repeat rows 1–2 to the desired length (noting that the finished tassel will be approx 30% longer than this measurement), ending with row 2.

- **Next row** (RS) k1 tbl * slip next st off the end of the needle and allow it to drop to the cast-on edge, p1, k1 tbl, repeat from * to end. [25 sts]
- **Row 1** p1 * k1 tbl, p1, repeat from * to end.
- **Row 2** k1 tbl, p1, k1 tbl, repeat from * to end.
- **Rows 3–12** work as rows 1–2 five times.
- Cut ribbon leaving a long end and pull through remaining sts and secure tightly. Stuff the top of the tassel and sew back seam. Wrap ribbon yarn around the base of the ball, and tie securely. Make a loop for the top.

Alternative embellishments

The tassel is quite beautiful in itself, however, it can easily be decorated with a contrasting texture or colour of ribbon yarn to tie it off. You could also add beads to weight the strands and change the look. Consider embroidering the top of the tassel or knitting it in a different colour altogether.

FRINGING

Fringing is a stranding of loose threads usually applied to the edges of projects. A plain design is brought to life with the use of fringing. A very fine ribbon fringe with heavy beads has a fluid feel, whereas a thicker ribbon with light beads has a tufted look.

COWBOY FRINGE

This is the kind of fringe you can get by using finer ribbon yarns. By keeping the knots and beads at the edge of the garment, you allow the thin ribbons to hang down for a sweeping, unusual style.

Cut a length of ribbon slightly more than twice the length of the finished fringe. Fold the strand in half and, using a crochet hook, draw the folded end through the edge of the knitted area where the fringing will be applied. Draw the loose ends of yarn through the loop, and pull them up firmly to form a knot. Once the fringing is completed, trim up the ends neatly.

Alternative embellishments

You can choose to leave the fringe very long (see example, right) or crop it shorter. Add small, contrasting beads (or sequins!) under the larger bead before the final knot is made. Tie some beads onto the bottom of the fringe as well to add weight and encourage movement. Try alternating the colour of the ribbons for a multihued effect.

BRUSH FRINGE

This technique uses a shorter, wider ribbon yarn and the fringe ends up being stiffer and thicker. This type of fringing uses multiple strands for each loop and ends are trimmed for a short, tufted look. Don't use a silky ribbon for this method. Use a large-size crochet hook to successfully draw through multiple strands.

Follow but adapt the directions for making up the Fine Fringe.

Alternative embellishments

This method of fringing can look very exciting when the ends of the strands are frayed. Substitute one of the strand multiples with a metallic ribbon for variety, or alternate a series of light and dark toned ribbons.

SHOW THEM OFF

Cowboy fringe

This type of fringe comes to life when used on the very edges of scarves and shawls. Use it on the bottom edges of bags to add character. Remember this type of edging for jackets and cuffs as well.

Brush fringe

Dress up an evening shawl or complete a smart clutch bag with a funky, brush-fringed top edge. Cushions look wonderful with this type of short, sharp fringe in a variety of colours.

BOWS

Bows are basic slipknots formed with ribbon, string, twine or other materials. They are practical knots when used, for instance, for gardening, but become decorative when used with ribbons.

A threaded bow can be both decorative as well as functional, if woven, for instance, into the waistband of a garment.

THREADED BOW

This type of bow demonstrates how a ribbon can be laced and threaded through a project, securing it with a bow. This can add a very feminine look to a design without changing the shaping. Only a series of equally spaced holes are needed in order to achieve this look.

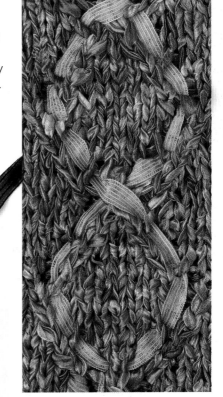

Alternative embellishments

For both methods of bow making, try threading beads onto the ribbon yarn before the ribbon is laced through the holes of the garment, or before it is finally tied into a bow. You could also knot beads onto the ends if the tie is going to be used as an adjustable waistband. Attach sequins to the individual bows or, for added lustre, use metallic thread for attaching.

FLOATING BOW

To make these fun, individual bows, knot them onto a small knitting needle or pencil and then slip them off the end. It's as easy as tying your shoelaces!

SHOW THEM OFF

The waistband is the perfect place to show off the threaded bow; however, a sleeve edge or a collar can also be pretty alternatives.

The floating bows are very versatile and can be randomly sprinkled over any garment, or stitched neatly onto a button band, collar or cuff.

CARING FOR RIBBON YARN GARMENTS

Care always needs to be taken with ribbon yarns because of their unique makeup. Each of them features different compositions and combinations of man-made and natural fibres. Consequently, washing your ribbon yarn garments is challenge. Once you understand the nature of your particular ribbon, however, washing your garments becomes a breeze.

Handwashing

Always use lukewarm water when handwashing. Make sure to dissolve your soap powder completely before you submerge your garments. When submerging, keep your ribbon yarn garment folded so that it keeps its shape. Keep it folded while it soaks and simply lightly agitate it while its in the water. It will then need one or two rinses in a new sinkful of lukewarm water to clean away the soap. Remember not to stretch out delicate ribbon yarns when removing the garment from the water. Be gentle and let the water drain away rather than lifting one particular section. Squeeze out any excess water and dry flat.

Machine washing

Before machine washing, pay particular attention to buttons or special features on your garment. If, for example, your ribbon yarn cardigan features hand-painted or hand-decorated buttons, you may have to remove them before machine washing. Another option would be to protect the whole garment in a pillowcase before washing. A great feature of ribbon yarns is that because they are unique combinations of natural and man-made fibres, they will be almost dry on the completion of a normal spin cycle. Fold them flat and leave them to finish drying naturally. To avoid stretching, do not hang your ribbon yarn items on hangers.

Dry cleaning

A structured item like a bag or anything with special delicate finishing, such as handmade buttons or an embellishment like a flower corsage, may pose a washing problem for you. In these cases, a visit to a reputable dry cleaners might be the perfect solution.

Ironing

If you are going to be pressing a ribbon yarn item with any type of nylon content, the item will need to be covered with muslin, a tea towel or a damp cloth before ironing, otherwise the material may melt.

FIBRE CONTENT

Below, you will find the fibre content of every yarn used in the projects. Use this information when formulating a plan for caring for your garments. When deciding on a particular project, it is wise to cross reference the ribbon yarn's fibre content to the care instructions so you can be aware that you will be able to machine wash the cardigan you have decided to knit, or if you are only going to be able to handwash it. This is important to know before you start the project: if it's something you don't want to have to spend too much time caring for, you are going to want to choose a substitute yarn

Colinette

Chrysalis	100% cotton
Enigma	55% cotton, 45% rayon
Giotto	50% cotton, 50% rayon

Crystal Palace

Deco Ribbon	70% acrylic, 30% nylon
Deco Stardust	55% lurex, 45% nylon
Mikado	50% cotton, 50% rayon
Party	100% nylon
Trio	50% nylon, 50% polyester

Lana Grossa

Bora Lux	80% microfibre, 20% polymide
Fresco	55% cotton, 45% polymide
India	68% microfibre, 32% cotton
Opaco Print	100% microfibre
Perla	60% microfibre, 20% viscose, 10% cotton, 10% silk
Twin Print	35% cotton, 30% acrylic, 30% viscose, 5% polymide

Trendsetter

Checkmate	80% polymide, 20% nylon
Pepita	86% polymide, 14% polyester
Segue	100% nylon

General ribbon yarn care notes

• *man-made and natural fibre blends*: A ribbon yarn blended with a combination of man-made and natural fibres will be more stable than a yarn that is 100% natural fibre. For instance, an acrylic and cotton blend is more durable than a 100% cotton ribbon yarn. Cotton and rayon blends can be washed on a gentle cycle and a low temperature in the machine unless they have a padding or lining. A cotton and polymide, or microfibre, blend is really resilient. Put these kinds of ribbon yarn garments in a cold temperature machine wash for best results. In a yarn where the majority of the fibres are man-made, handwash the finished garment at a cool temperature.

• *natural fibres*: 100% cotton is quite resilient and can be washed in a cool temperature machine wash to avoid shrinkage.

• *man-made fibres*: Nylon is a funny material that you can wash in a machine but never on a hot temperature or else there is a danger the item will melt. Wash nylon only on a cool temperature in a gentle cycle. For a totally man-made ribbon yarn, such as an acrylic and polyester blend, handwash the garment using a soft detergent made especially for handwashing. Remember that a completely man-made ribbon yarn will be unstable when washed at a high temperature, therefore, always handwash these items in cool water. Acrylic and nylon blends are suitable for a gentle handwash or a delicate machine wash.

RESOURCES

UNITED KINGDOM

COLINETTE YARNS

EAST

Arts & Crafts
Tunstead Road
Hoveton
Wroxham
Norfolk, NR12 8QG
Tel: 01603 783505

D & P Colchester
The Barn
South Lodge Farm
Low Road
Great Plumstead
Norwich
Norfolk, NR13 5ED
Tel: 01603 721466

EAST MIDLANDS

Taylor's Teddies
4a Graham Road
Great Malvern
Worcestershire
WR14 2HN
Tel: 01684 572760

Bee Inspired Limited
The Old Post Office
236 Windmill Avenue
Kettering
Northants, NN1 7DQ
Tel: 01536 514646

Belinda Bramhall
The Knitting Workshop
23 Trowell Grove
Long Eaton
Nottingham, NG10 4A
Tel: 0115 9468370

Quorn Country Crafts
18 Churchgate
Loughborough
Leicestershire, LE11 1UD
Tel: 01509 211604

NORTH EAST/YORKSHIRE

Jenny Scott's Creative Embroidery
The Old Post Office
39 Duke Street
Settle
North Yorkshire
BD24 9DJ
Tel: 01729 824298

Noctule
50 Gillygate
York
North Yorkshire
YO31 7EQ
Tel: 01904 610043

Attica 2
Commercial Street
Hebden Bridge
West Yorkshire
HX7 8AJ

Bobbins
Wesley Hall
Church Street
Whitby
North Yorkshire, YO22 4DE
Tel: 01947 600585

Busy Hands
Unit 16, Ashbrook Park
Parkside Lane
Leeds, LS11 5SF
Tel: 0113 2720851

SOUTH EAST

Portmeadow Designs
104 Walton Street
Oxford
Oxon, OX2 6EB
Tel: 01865 311008

Burford Needlecraft
117 High Street
Burford
Oxon, OX18 4RG
Tel: 01993 822136

The Knit Tin
2 Fountain Court
Olney
Bucks, MK46 4BB
Tel: 01234 714300

Yummies
91 Queens Park Road
Brighton
East Sussex, BN2 0GJ
Tel: 01273 672632

Kangaroo
70 High Street
Lewes
East Sussex, BN7 1XG
Tel: 01273 478554

Irene Noad
1 Farnham Road
Bishops Stortford
Herts, CM23 1JJ
Tel: 01279 653701

Thread Bear
350 Limpsfield Road
South Croydon
CR2 9BX
Tel: 0208 6575050

Creations
79 Church Road
Barnes
London, SW13 9HH

Creations
29 Turnham Green Terrace
Chiswick
London, W4 1RG

Loop
41 Cross Street
London, N1 2BB
Tel: 020 7288 1160

Myfanwy Hart
Winifred Cottage
17 Elms Road
Fleet
Hants, GU15 3EG
Tel: 01252 617667

SOUTH WEST

Cottage Yarns
Glebe Land
Aveton
Gifford
Kingsbridge
Devon, TQ7 4LX
Tel: 01548 550741

Sally Carr Designs
The Yarn Shop
31 High Street
Totnes
Devon, TQ9 5NP
Tel: 01803 863060

The Wool & Craft Shop Ltd.
Swanage
Dorset, BH19 1AB
Tel: 01929 422814

WEST MIDLANDS

Web of Wool
53 Regent Grove
Holly Walk
Leamington Spa
Warwick, CV32 4PA
Tel: 01926 311614

Cucumberpatch Limited
13 March Avenue
Wolstanton
Newcastle-under-Lyme
Staffordshire, ST5 8BB
Tel: 01782 878234

K2Tog
97 High Street
Wolstanton
Newcastle under Lyme
Staffordshire, ST5 0EP
Tel: 01782 862332

Natural Knits
Hoar Park Craft Village
B4114 Ansley
Warwickshire, CV10 0QU
Tel: 0121 7487981

NORTH WEST

Victoria Grant
Waterways
High Street
Uppermill
Oldham
Lancashire, OL3 6HT
Tel: 01457 870756

Marchmoon Limited
73 Avondale Road
Liverpool
Merseyside, L15 3HF
Tel: 01704 577415

WALES

B's Hive
20–22 Church Street
Monmouth
Gwent, NP25 3BU
Tel: 01600 713548

SCOTLAND

Wooly Ewe
7 Abbey Court
Kelso
Berwickshire
Scotland, TD5 7JA
Tel: 01573 225889

Ragamuffin
278 Canon Gate
The Royal Mile
Edinburgh
Scotland, EH8 8AA
Tel: 0131 5576007

Fibres
133 Commercial Street
Lerwick
Shetland
Scotland, ZE1 0DL
Tel: 01595 695575

Victoria Gibson
The Esplanade
Lerwick
Shetland
Scotland, ZE1 0LL
Tel: 01595 692816

C E Cross Stitch
Narvik
Weyland Terrace
Kirkwall, Orkney
Scotland, KW15 1LS
Tel: 01856 879049

Hume Sweet Hume
Pierowall Village
Westray
Orkney
Scotland, KW17 2DH
Tel: 01857 677259

Elizabeth Lovick
Harbour View
Front Road
Orkney
Scotland, KW17 2SL
Tel: 01603 783505

Unlimited Colour Company
2a Latheron Lane
Ullapool
Wester-ross
Scotland, IV26 2XB
Tel: 01854 612844

Patterns of Light
Kishorn Shop
Kishorn
Strathcarron
Wester-ross
Scotland, IV54 8XB
Tel: 01520 733363

Phoenix Centre
The Park
Findliorn Bay
Forres
Moray
Scotland, IV36 0TZ
Tel: 01309 690110

The Knitting Parlour
The Park
Findliorn Bay
Forres
Moray
Scotland, IV36 0TZ
Tel: 01684 527760

Pie in the Skye
Ferry View
Armadale Bay
Sleat
Isle of Skye
Scotland, IV45 8RS
Tel: 01471 844370

Di Gilpin
Hansa Close
Burghers Close
141 South Street
St Andrews, Fife
Scotland, KY16 9UN
Tel: 01334 476193

The Wool Shed
Alford Heritage Centre
Mart Road, Alford
Aberdeenshire
Scotland, AB33 8BZ
Tel: 01975 562906

Galloway Knitwear
6 Manx View
Port William
Dumfries & Galloway
Scotland, DG8 9SA
Tel: 01988 700789

SOUTH WEST

Divine Design
Libra Court
Fore Street
Sidmouth
Devon, EX10 8AJ
Tel: 07967 127 273

Knitting Corner
9 Pepper Street
Tavistock
Devon, PL19 0BD
Tel: 01822 617410

Hayes Wool
149-150 East Reach
Taunton
Somerset, TA1 3HT
Tel: 01823 284768

NORTHERN IRELAND

Coolwoolz
46 Mill Hill
Warringstown
Co. Down, BT66 7QP
Tel: 02838 820202

CRYSTAL PALACE YARNS
Distributed in the UK by
Hantex Ltd., Jacqui and Paul
Smith
http://www.hantex.co.uk/

LANA GROSSA

EAST MIDLANDS

Heirs and Graces
The Square
Bakewell
Derbyshire, DE45 1DA
Tel: 01629 815873
Fax: 01629 815873
www.patchworkdirect.com

NORTH EAST

Village Craft Shop
37 North Road
Boldon Colliery
Tyne & Wear, NE35 8AZ
Tel: 0191 519 1645

SOUTH EAST

Shoreham Knitting & Needlecraft
19 East Street
Shoreham-by-Sea
West Sussex, BN43 5ZE
Tel: 01273 461029
Fax: 01273 465407
www.englishyarns.co.uk

Battle Wool Shop
2 Mount Street
Battle
East Sussex, TN33 OEG
Tel: 01424 775073

Taj Yarn & Crafts
2 Wellesey Avenue
Richings Park
Iver
Buckinghamshire, S10 9AY
Tel: 01753 653900

Loop
41 Cross Street
Islington
London, N1 2BB
Tel: 020 7288 1160
Fax: 020 7288 1160
www.loop.gb.com

Gades
Victoria Plaza
242 Churchill South
Southend on Sea
Essex, SS2 5SD
Tel: 01702 613789

Pandora
196 High Street
Guildford
Surrey, GU1 3HZ
Tel: 01483 572558

Fax: 01483 450903
www.stitch1knit1.com

WEST MIDLANDS

Knit 2 together
97 High Street
Wolstanton
Newcastle-under-Lyme
Staffordshire, ST5 0EP
Tel: 01782 862332
www.cucumberpatch.co.uk

NORTH WEST

Spinning A Yarn
46 Market Street
Ulverston
Cumbria, LA12 7LS
Tel: 01229 581020
www.spinningayarn.com

Stash
Godstall House
4 Godstall Lane
Chester
Cheshire, CH1 1LN
Tel: 01244 311136
www.celticove.com

And Sew What
247 Eaves Lane
Chorley
Lancashire, PR6 0AG
Tel: 01257 267438
www.sewwhat.gb.com

Fun 2 Do
21 Scotch Street
Carlisle
Cumbria, CA3 8PY
Tel: 01228 523843
Fax: 01228 523483
www.fun2do.co.uk

SCOTLAND

Cormack's and Crawford's
56-57 High Street
Dingwall
Ross-shire
Scotland, IV15 9HL
Tel: 01349 562234
Fax: 01349 865448

Di Gilpin
Hansa Close, Burghers Close
141 South Street
St. Andrews
Fife
Scotland, KY16 9UN
Tel: 01334 476193
www.handknitwear.com

HK Handknit
83 Bruntsfield Place
Edinburgh
Scotland, EH10 4HG
Tel: 0131 228 1551
www.handknit.co.uk

The Wool Shed
Alford Heritage Centre
Mart Road
Alford
Aberdeenshire
Scotland, AB33 8BZ
Tel: 01975 562806

Twist Fibre Craft Studio
88 High Street
Newburgh
Cupar, Fife
Scotland, KY14 6AQ
Tel: 01337 842843
Fax: 01337 842843
www.twistfibrecraft.co.uk

Woolcrafts Studio
Springhill Farm
Coldingham Moor Road
Eyemouth
Berwickshire
Scotland, TD14 5TX

ROWAN YARNS
For further information call
Rowan Yarns direct on:
+ 44 (0) 1484 681 881 or visit
their website:
www.knitrowan.com

TRENDSETTER YARNS
Suppliers willing to mail order
to countries outside the US.

Trendsetter Mail Order
16745 Saticoy St. #101
C/O Customer Service-Retail
Van Nuys
California 91406
Tel: (818)780-5497
www.Trendsetteryarns.com

The Yarn Lady
24371 Ave. De La Carlotta
Laguna Hills
California 92653
Tel: (949)770-7809
www.Yarnlady.com

Great Yarns
4023 Rucker Avenue
Everett, Washington 98201
Tel: (425)252-8155
www.Greatyarns.com

Desert Designs
5100 Beltline Road
Dallas, Texas 75254
Tel: (972)392-9276

Great Balls of Yarn
319 Belvedere Road
W. Palm Beach
Florida 33405
Tel: (561)651-1225
www.Greatballsofyarn.com

AUSTRALIA

LION BRAND YARNS

The Knitting Loft
PO Box 266
Tunstall Square
East Doncaster, VIC 3109
Australia
Tel: +61 3 9841 4818
Fax: +61 3 9841 4818
Email: sales@knittingloft.com
http://www.knittingloft.com

TRENDSETTER YARNS

Threads and More
141 Boundary Road
Bardon, QLD 4065
Tel: +61 7 3367 0864
Fax: +61 7 3367 0458
Email:
shop@threadsandmore.com.au
www.threadsandmore.com.au

GENERAL YARN SUPPLIERS

Yarns Galore
5/25 Queens Road
Mount Pleasant, WA 6153
Tel: +61 8 9315 3070
Fax: +61 8 9315 3070
http://yarnsgalore.com.au

Xotix Yarns
PO Box 1636
Kingscliff
NSW 2487
Australia
Tel: +61 2 6677 7241
Fax: +61 2 6677 7418
www.xotixyarns.com.au

Cleckheaton
Head Office: Australian
Country Spinners Pty Ltd.
314 Albert Street
Brunswick
VIC 3056
Tel: +61 3 9380 3888
Fax: +61 3 9387 2674
http://www.cleckheaton.biz

NEW ZEALAND

LION BRAND YARNS

Dyepot
Accent Fibres
1084 Maraekakaho Road
R.D.5
Hastings
Hawkes Bay
New Zealand
Tel/fax: +64 6 876 4233
Email: Sheryl@dyepot.co.nz
http://www.dyepot.co.nz

INDEX

CREDITS

All photos and illustrations are the copyright of Quarto Publishing plc.

While every effort has been made to credit contributors, Quarto would like to apologise should there have been any omissions or errors—and would be pleased to make the appropriate correction for future editions of the book.